War of Deception

... the facts and fallacies
about the war in Iraq

War of Deception

... the facts and fallacies about the war in Iraq

DAIM ZAINUDDIN

Pelanduk Publications
www.pelanduk.com

Published by
Pelanduk Publications (M) Sdn Bhd
(Co. No. 113307-W)
12 Jalan SS13/3E,
Subang Jaya Industrial Estate
47500 Subang Jaya
Selangor Darul Ehsan, Malaysia

Address all correspondence to
Pelanduk Publications (M) Sdn Bhd
P.O. Box 8265, 46785 Kelana Jaya
Selangor Darul Ehsan, Malaysia
website: *www.pelanduk.com*
e-mail: *rusaone@tm.net.my*

Perpustakaan Negara Malaysia   Cataloguing-in-Publication Data

Daim Zainuddin, Tun, 1938-
War of deception : ... the facts and fallacies about the war in Iraq / Daim Zainuddin.
ISBN 967-978-883-0
1. Iraq War, 2003–Deception. 2. Iraq War, 2003–Causes.
3. Iraq–Politics and government–2003-. I. Title.
956.70443

Printed and bound in Malaysia

I thank Allah, the Almighty,
in whose hands lies all guidance.

This book is dedicated to the people of Iraq
and to those who cherish peace and freedom.

Contents

Prologue

"When valour preys on reasons, it eats the sword it fights with."

William Shakespeare

"We're not only a powerful nation. We're also a compassionate nation ... we cry for the orphan. We care for the mom who is alone."

George W. Bush, in Africa, July 2003

I OPPOSED the Iraq War by writing and by joining a protest march. I now hope the occupiers will restore order, revive the shattered economy of Iraq and go home. Is that plausible?

We all hope Iraq will not be a protracted conflict. Our news senses are numbed when conflicts drag on and on. That is when we are resigned to expecting peace efforts to fail, when deaths are reduced to statistics. That will be the height of despair. In that sense, Iraq must not turn out to be another Afghanistan. Iraq is not a failed State.

The overriding priority is to let Iraqis get on with their lives. It outweighs all the recriminations—the debate on

American Imperialism, hegemony, hints of a clash of civilisations, speculations on whether Saudi Arabia had been the real target and the question of legitimacy triggered by the near-solo effort by the United States to invade and occupy Iraq. The intellectual debate will take its course.

This is a paradox we have to come to terms with—the occupation of Iraq is illegal, but the reconstruction must succeed.

As for the U.S. and Britain, winning the peace in Iraq and the hearts and minds of Iraqis is far more complicated than winning an election back home. Firstly, Iraqis who prodded the U.S. to invade were mainly exiles, dissidents and separatists. Ahmad Chalabi of the Iraqi National Congress (INC) left the country with his family in 1958. There was no way to find out what local Iraqis think, until after the war. Now, indications are that many of them are opposing the occupation. Secondly, quality of life has not improved. *The Washington Post* (August 11, 2003) quoted one Tha'ara Amar, a shopkeeper in the city of Amarah, as saying: "We have no fuel, no water, no electricity for days. Children are dying in hospitals."

Thirdly, the occupiers wish they could present a kinder and gentler form of authority as opposed to Saddam Hussein's reign of terror, as they put it. This benign authority concept has quickly floundered in part because the occupiers are trying to weed out Saddam's sympathisers. The elimination process has the Americans roughing out the Iraqis, subjecting them to such humiliating act as bowing their heads to the ground. This was the case during the Vietnam War when "men were reduced to abject humiliation and powerlessness in front of their families," wrote James L. Larocca, who served in Vietnam and is now a professor of public policy.

Such degradation has sparked retaliations in Iraq. There is a mini rebellion. It creates a vicious cycle. On April 28, 2003, for example, U.S. soldiers shot at demonstrators in Fallujah, killing 18 Iraqis and wounding 78. And lastly, the occupiers must find or, rather, kill Saddam at all costs.

The famous Robert Fisk of *The Independent* newspaper reported on Aug. 6: "two families, most of them children, 21 in all, were blasted to pieces in the village of Ajwa when the Americans bombed their homes on April 2 in the hope of killing Saddam".

Then, on July 27, 2003, the American troops opened fire at a crowded street in the Mansour district, killing 11 including two children, their mother and crippled father. Fear and paranoia could have morphed into state terrorism-like acts.

Such actions have radicalised segments of the populations. Thus, by the time Uday, Qusay and his 14-year-old son were killed, the local public opinion has shifted. An email sent out by an American soldier serving in Iraq sums up the situation succinctly. "Somewhere down the line, we became an occupation force in (Iraqi) eyes. We don't feel like heroes any more" was the email written by Isaac Kindblade of the 671st Engineer Company and quoted by *The Guardian* newspaper. Others now resent both Saddam Hussein and George Bush.

Still, it did not help when the unloved Americans and Britons celebrated the gruesome deaths of Saddam Hussein's sons and grandchild. Tony Blair greeted their deaths as "great news". *The New York Times* called the killing of Uday and Qusay "the most encouraging news out of Iraq in weeks." To *The Washington Post,* the deaths represented "a very serious blow to the diehard resistance that has plagued the postwar administration."

Uday and Qusay were trapped in a small villa. Instead of flushing them out, they were hit with at least seven anti-tank missiles. A senior U.S. military officer said the Americans had to act decisively as there could have been secret escape routes from the villa. That can be refuted. If there were secret tunnels and such Uday and Qusay would have fled. In 1989 Uday bludgeoned to death a servant at a party given in honour of Hosni Mubarak's wife, prompting the Egyptian president to call him a psychopath. There were other unverified horrific tales.

Was that the American justice that we saw of the barely recognisable bodies of Uday and Qusay that had to be "touched up"? Note the use of euphemisms. These constitute attempts to decriminalise various U.S. actions.

During the three-week invasion, the Americans, British and Australians unleashed 30,000 air strikes killing thousands of Iraqi civilians. Each bombing run cost $15,000. There are 300,000 coalition troops in the Middle East, half the number saw action.

During the invasion, the *Time* magazine showed the picture of a U.S. marine proudly wearing his helmet with a skull and a crossbow and "Kill 'em all" spelt out in dripping blood-red letters. It is hardly the language of a compassionate liberator when the instruction was: "If you see an Iraqi in civilian clothes coming towards you, even with a stick—shoot!" *Daily Mirror* carried the views of Lance Corporal Steven Gerrard on the American pilot whose not-so-friendly fire killed his mate. Steven Gerrard said: "He had absolutely no regard for human life. He was a cowboy, he had just gone out on a folly." Are the Americans as the paragon of democracy incapable of terror? Are we to accept that the Americans kill and terrorise purely in self defence to advance the cause of freedom and democracy? The truth is they commit their fair share of atrocities, those that will shape the impressionable minds of the young Iraqis now seemingly enjoying the spectacle.

As a Muslim I don't wish the Americans more torment and violent death. There had been enough suffering. The Americans are being killed too although the number seen as mere statistics, are negligible when compared to the 57,000 U.S. troops who died in the 1959-1975 Vietnam War. But things are not getting any better in Iraq. On August 19, 2003, the top U.N. envoy in Iraq, Sergio Vieira de Mello was killed with 20 others when a massive truck bomb ripped apart the U.N. headquarters in Baghdad.

George Bush retains considerable support for invading Iraq but clearly the young Americans expecting to go home soon after the war have been seized by fright. Rather playfully, *The Economist* of August 16, 2003 had a cover story that read "Show me the way to go home". Now, Deputy Prime Minister Datuk Seri Abdullah Ahmad Badawi's remarks at the time of the invasion that "this is a black mark in history" can be seen in the fuller context.

Undeniably, the Iraqi adventure was a culmination of decades of U.S.'s efforts to influence events and decisions in the Middle East. Now it has a piece of volatile Arab land. That effectively makes the U.S. a part of the Middle East, a member of the Arab Club. Seats reserved for Iraq in Arab League and OPEC meetings should technically and yes, bizarrely be occupied by their American rulers.

Not that the Arab leaders are splitting hairs over this tragic loss of sovereignty. Either they have been kept out of the arguments, or they willfully opted out.

Day by day, the Americans are dangerously liable to succumb to their own propaganda that the Iraqi resistance will dissipate once Iraqis are convinced that Saddam and his two sons have been eliminated. The Americans are wrong to suggest that those shooting at their soldiers in Iraq are saboteurs, Baathist elements and remnants of Saddam Hussein's supporters. The resistance is also intertwined with anti-Americanism, interwoven with humiliation and hopelessness. The Iraqis regard the Americans as conquerors and they have in history encountered invaders of all kind. According to Ahmed S. Hashim, professor of strategic studies at the U.S. Naval War College Newport, Rhode Island,[1] various resistance groups had "come out of the woodwork". Saddam and Baath loyalists are fighting the occupiers. There are others, nationalists, patriotic individuals and insurgent groups who "resent the U.S. presence and are angered by the U.S. failure to restore law, order and security and by U.S. methods of operation, which are seen as deliberately humiliating to the Iraqis and their honor". Paradoxically, Islamists liberated from decades of suppression are also haunting their American "liberators". On paper, the war in Iraq was still an extension to the war on terror. Instead, post-Saddam Iraq may well be a breeding ground for *jihad*.[2]

---

1 *The Daily Star Online*, "Insurgency is no monolith" posted on July 28, 2003

2 *The New Yorker* of Sept. 16, 2002, "The man behind bin Laden—How an Egyptian doctor became a master of terror," traced the roots and causes of the Jihad movement, albeit from a Western viewpoint.

Saddam was not the nicest of characters; he brought much suffering to the population. But to assign all the blame for the muddle in Iraq on Saddam will be a gross miscalculation. As the occupiers who invaded Iraq without the backing of the international community, the Americans cannot afford to make such mistakes. Now, the international community should call on the Americans to bring Saddam to justice, not to parade, and this is a prayer, his charred remains or something. To achieve peace by savage means is to breed future conflicts and suicide bombers.

For the long-suffering Iraqis to get on with their lives, the Americans must succeed. If the Americans genuinely want to bring freedom and democracy, that is. We can cheer their hasty retreat if it comes to that, but if that means plunging Iraq into total anarchy, that is a dreadful wish. Opposing the war, wishing Iraqis and the occupiers well in the reconstruction mission all represent higher values.

Will the Americans deliver on the promise and go home? We shall see. We can give them the benefit of the doubt while making our feelings known and articulate our thoughts forcefully. To be effective, the Arab and Muslim World must be learned and sensible. The Arab media, I believe, should now be preoccupied with substantive discussions—to calmly and intelligently tell the Americans where they had gone wrong and to churn out ideas. Pile up the pressure. Write to the American Press. Talk to their journalists, lobby groups and diplomats. Organise peaceful marches. Arabs and Muslims must protest intelligently. The white man's burden drivel is not dead because many whites still think they are superior and the others badly need their leadership. This is a scourge we must fight sensibly.

The upshot is that Iraq's economic success will be a liberating force. This shall be an escape from the despair that has tormented Arabs in the last 100 years. In a way, it is pointless to quibble over the real intentions of the occupiers. They pursue their interests unashamedly. They fit into a neat pattern. The British had after World War I created Arab countries, which, in their words were "weak and pliable". They called this "Arab Facade." When the United States displaced the British and to a certain extent the French as the dominant player in the region, they just fit into the framework. Now both are in Iraq, telling Iraqis the day of their "liberation", that is the fall of Saddam Hussein's regime, April 9, shall be a National holiday.[3]

While the Americans swiftly foisted upon Iraqis new milestones to celebrate, the jury is still out on the central issue of why was Iraq invaded. No straightforward answer has been forthcoming. No Weapons of Mass Destruction (WMD), the sole trigger-point for the invasion, have been discovered. Neither was it a plausible follow-up to the war on terror. In fact the Iraqi invasion had complicated the war on terror.

By now rival senior politicians in U.S. and Britain have been trading insults, and openly accusing George Bush and Tony Blair of lying, at the very least of a poor judgment. Some Americans are blaming Blair for influencing them to go to war. Arab intellectuals, British politicians and left-leaning American and British journalists and writers have all tried to get Bush and Blair not to go to war. George Galloway, a Brit-

---

3 Tamim Al-Barghouti, a Palestinian poet living in Cairo, called the decision "utterly stupid" in an article "America, like Napoleon, takes colonialism to absurd lengths", for the *Daily Star Online* (Lebanon).

ish MP from Blair's Labour Party, had warned that Iraq could be Blair's Suez—the popular British PM, Anthony Eden lost his job in the wake of the 1956 Suez Crisis.

For the first time since coming into office in 1997, Blair appeared vulnerable and is seen by segments of his Labour Party as a liability. Lord (Dennis) Healey, a former Labour Chancellor and Defence Secretary during Harold Wilson's and James Callaghan's administrations, has urged Blair to step aside for Chancellor Gordon Brown.

Healey and others believe that Blair's undoing was the undiminished zeal to please the Americans and to have his place in history. Instead of earning plaudits, Blair has been confronted with a major crisis sparked by the death of Dr David Kelly.

Kelly, who did manage to send an email to a journalist friend to warn of "many dark actors playing games", was said to be the source of a story by the BBC's Andrew Gilligan on Downing Street "sexing up" the actual threat of Iraq's WMD. Gilligan subsequently wrote in the *Daily Mail* that it was Blair's director of communications Alastair Campbell who had spiced up the allegations. Kelly was head of biological inspectors of the U.N. mission, UNSCOM. Between 1991 and 1998, he went to Iraq 37 times. The episode was central in the debate on the justifications for the invasion. I am amazed that nobody actually asked if Alastair Campbell did not put in the bit on Iraq being able to assemble dangerous weapons in 45 minutes, who, then was the culprit? Was Dr David Kelly a whistle blower?

The liberal newspapers in Britain that would ordinarily back a Labour Government have turned on the heat on Blair. Even the *Financial Times* and *The Economist* (which supported the war) are suggesting that the Hutton Inquiry has hurt the Blair Government. Soon after his superior and friend Tony Blair was grilled at the Inquiry, Alastair Campbell announced his resignation. We are not convinced the culture of spin and the emphasis on presentation will change though.

It is unmistakable that public disquiet in America and Britain has been on the rise. The American troops are fretting openly. They want to go home. A more fatal consequence is a full-scale Iraqi rebellion. The Americans must be forewarned of the uprising fuelled by the earlier "liberation" of Baghdad in 1917 by the troops of British Lt.-General Stanley Maude. Maude, too, received a warm reception as illustrated in a dispatch by an "embedded" *Guardian* newspaper at that time. Instead an uprising erupted. The British bombed and gassed the "miscreants", killing 10,000. One Sheikh Dhari who had in 1920 killed Colonel Gerard Leachman is a legend for his "feat". His descendants are now calling Iraqis to unite to resist the "American occupiers". An earlier American intervention in the 1980s did not end on a happy note, illuminating another Arab character—they have a resistance streak. American troops had arrived in Beirut to act as a buffer between the militias. They bolted after 241 marines were killed when a suicide bomber blew up their barracks in October 1983.

These days only the American casualties matter. In Iraq, as in Vietnam, Beirut, Gulf War I and elsewhere, American lives appear to have far greater value than the civilians who perished in conflicts involving the Americans. Consciously, the *New York Daily News* published a letter from a reader, who said: "For every GI killed, 20 Iraqis must be executed."

Based on a survey by the *Associated Press* in June 2003, some 3,240 civilians died in the three-week war. On a single day of clashes after war officially ended, some 100 were killed. Post-war Iraq has seen lawlessness reigned, pent-up sentiments unleashed and thus more killing.

By being high-handed, the Americans will fuel more anger, which is not going to be doused by more tough talk and threats. "We must stay tough", said a bellicose George Bush trying to rally the troops from Africa. A United Nations peacekeeping force from Muslim countries is what Iraq needs. The Americans will pacify many angry Muslim souls by allowing Muslim troops to patrol the streets. However, Muslim nations will generally not want to commit as peacekeepers unless they go there under the U.N. banner. For this to happen, the U.S. will have to go to the U.N. as Prime Minister Datuk Seri Dr Mahathir Mohamad correctly pointed out. Belatedly and somewhat reluctantly, and after all the tragic deaths and killings, the U.S. indicated that it would accept a U.N.-sponsored force provided it is led by an American commander. The U.S. has since returned to the U.N. over Iraq, willing to share but not relinquish control of post-war reconstruction.

In the meantime, the more Paul Bremer acts imperial, the more harm he will bring to the American troops. When he arrived in May 2003, Bremer scrapped plans for a National Assembly to choose an interim Government. He said the Iraqi opposition was too disorganised.

Such condescension stokes up the Iraqi resistance. Bremer responded with a curt warning: "We are going to fight them and impose our will on them and we will capture or kill them until we have imposed law and order in this country."

Iraq has a strong middle class. The middle class will have some influence over the rest. They need to be convinced they have a say in the affairs of their country. The doctors and professionals interviewed by the BBC are none too pleased with the goings-on. The American troops cannot conceivably keep the peace by occupying palaces and important buildings in town. They will be a rallying point for Iraqi resistance.

There may not yet be a quagmire, truly a dreaded word, but the hostilities have derailed the intended reconstruction. For the Iraqi economy to rebound, oil must flow. Yet the oilfields are burning. The Americans must, however, show their sincerity by inviting a broad mix of oil companies into Iraq, including Arab and Muslim oil companies. A reluctance to do so will deepen and confirm the suspicion that the U.S. is after Iraqi oil. Iraq needs peace and new investments.

Events have not proceeded according to the American script. They are caught in the WMD debate. The American and British intelligence have been mocked. It seems that American intelligence had been fed half-truths and untruths by Iraqi exiles and officials of the Iraqi National Congress bent on ousting Saddam Hussein. Intelligence, according to James Woosley, a former CIA director, is all about filling in the jigsaw puzzle, or guesswork. They should not invade a country based on guesswork.

If the rest of the world chose to be horrified at this web of deception, it will be in vain. Tall tales about Iraq's quick-fire ability to build WMD in 45 minutes,[4] the uranium oxide sup-

---

4 This dramatic claim made it into a dossier presented by British Government in the run-up to the War.

ply from Niger,[5] and the Jessica Lynch caper,[6] had been preceded by real gems.

When both George Bush and Tony Blair insisted that the "evidence" of weapons of mass destruction (WMD) or at the very least the evidence of "products" or a "programme" of WMD[7] would soon materialise, they were simply regurgitating Ronald Reagan's lines. That was in 1981 when the Reagan Administration cooked up a story about "Libyan hitmen roaming the streets of Washington to assassinate Reagan."[8] The media frenzy ensued. Reagan, former actor, said then: "We have the evidence and (Muammar Gaddafi) knows it". By 1986 the serial-lying machine spewed new tales. Gaddafi, said *The Wall Street Journal*, was planning new terrorist attacks on the U.S. and that the two countries were on a collision course. Hedrick Smith wrote in *Power Game* that the story was planted. The image of Gaddafi, branded by Reagan as the "mad dog of the Middle East" has since softened, especially now that there has been agreement in the long-running battle over the 1988 bombing of a Pan-Am airliner over Lockerbie, Scotland that cost 270 lives. Libya will pay a total of $2.7 billion in compensation. To be in the good books of the U.S.,

---

5 Both Britain and the U.S. cited this to strengthen their case for war.

6 The 19-year old Private was a major celebrity during the Iraq War; she was supposed to be captured by the Iraqis but was miraculously rescued. The BBC World reported on July 10 that U.S. Army has disapproved the dramatic tale; she was apparently injured in a road accident and had been rescued by Iraqi Medics. She is now prepared to give her version of the story for $1 million.

7 By July, sensing the torrent of condemnations of the WMD claims, both U.S. and Britain started to lower expectations. They spoke of products and programme of WMD instead of WMD proper.

8 Noam Chomsky, *Pirates and Emperors, Old and New: International Terrorism in the Real World*, South End Press, Cambridge, Mass., 2002

Libya must still prove that it has no intention of developing weapons of mass destruction and to do more to show that it has "abandoned terrorism".

Saddam's Iraq faced similar charges. Iraq never had any nuclear weapon which meant George Bush's determination to rid Saddam of the most lethal weapon[9] was all hot air. The propaganda machine's choice of Niger as the bogus supplier of uranium to Saddam Hussein's Iraq, was in my mind deliberate. With the Lost Continent in a state of perpetual chaos, who would have been bothered to check, seemed to be the grand idea.

Indeed, the exploitation of Africa in the propaganda war makes the deception-strategy more depraved. The intensity of the war on terror has brought into sharper focus the American foreign policy elsewhere including in Africa. I know Africa pretty well. Not too long before the currency speculators devastated the Tiger economies of Asia in 1997, four African presidents told me that squeamish Westerners were troubled by the sizeable Malaysian investments in their countries. It seemed that the West was content to let Africa degenerate but others should not help either. The African leaders warned me when I called on them that Malaysian investors were being watched and might be smeared. Ghana's Jerry Rawlings was most animated when I spoke to him on the grounds of the presidential palace in Accra. The Africans had warmed up to the Malaysian investors. We were seen to be nicer by comparison to their colonial masters who continued to exploit African resources. The African leaders said the

9 The BBC (July 10, 2003) quoted Gred Thielman, recently retired senior U.S. intelligence officer, as saying that Iraq had no nuclear weapon.

West feared that Malaysians would teach Africans to be more disciplined.

Some years had lapsed. Guinean President Lansana Conte is ill. He was indeed a chain-smoker. His Muslim nation has since plunged into a civil war said to be fomented by American-educated former President of Liberia Charles Taylor, also indicted for war crimes by an international court in neighbouring Sierra Leone. Financing the civil wars and mayhem had been the illegal diamond trade.

Throughout this war on terror reign (they all say it will take decades), the despairing Africans were left to slaughter each other or to die of AIDS. International peacekeepers went to a few troubled spots, and that was it. We saw on television "rebels" or "Government troops" shooting insouciantly at crowds. The young famished. Towns ravaged.

Then overnight, President George Bush got interested in AIDS and the African despair. I applaud his condemnation of the slave trade. I had toured Gore Island that is now a tourist site. I applaud Bush's concern for the dying AIDS victims.

What troubled me was this terrible coincidence of Bush's African interest—was this yet another deception to please Black voters?

Bush should have gone to Mozambique where all the African leaders had assembled for a major regional meeting. He could have met everyone including the presidents of Burkina Faso and Mali who wrote to *The New York Times* about how the rich countries' subsidies to their cotton producers—$5.8 billion a production year—is strangling them. The annual European Union subsidy for each cow of $913 per annum, is greater than the average income of a sub-Saharan African at $490 per annum. Japan's subsidy is $2,700 per cow.

Interestingly, Bush's concern for Africa's interest started with the war on terror. Bush was persuaded to visit Africa partly to make sure the impoverished nations do not turn into breeding ground for "terrorism". At a broader level, the war on terror has re-ignited interests on the intricacies of world affairs and politics.

The war on terror has presented the world hyper-power with a rude awakening. They are not well liked around the world as surveys have illustrated. As those who shape American foreign policy fine-tune their strategies, I think they are unlikely to worry about public opinion. Some have argued that while one million Algerians died to win Independence from the French, decades later one million Algerians poured to the streets to greet visiting French President Jacques Chirac. Perhaps Algeria would have fared better if it had not been colonialised. It is understandable now for many Algerians to seek to migrate to France given the economic disparities between the two countries. Throughout the world, people migrate to improve their lot. Migrant workers reportedly remit home $66 billion a year. Some give a higher estimate. Colonisation and domination are no less evil if the colonised are attracted to the lifestyle of their colonial masters.

Will mankind be subject to more domination and subjugation? Indeed if the Cold War was the Third World War, and clash of civilisations involving Islam is the Fourth World War, then the Fifth World War shall revolve around Confucius. China is set to become an economic power, Tony Blair acknowledged as much in his July 2003 trip to China. Blair, optimistically, mentioned a 10-year for China to overtake the rest. I think it may take a bit longer given that China is a huge country in various stages of development.

Blair was also condescending, said an *Independent* columnist, in the manner he addressed the university students. He treated the elite students as if they are in primary school, complained the columnist Yasmin Alibhai-Brown. China is strong in history, culture and civilisation, Blair should have known better.

Finally, with some changes, this book and the words could have been written anytime in the past. Motives and conflicts have not changed. A character in a new novel set in Afghanistan, observed wryly: "Back then, the Soviets said they were fighting *basmachi*, bandits backed by Pakistani intelligence and the CIA. Today, the Americans say they are fighting terrorism. In many cases, they were the same people."[10]

---

[10] John Fullerton, *A Hostile Place*, Macmillan, London, 2003

Chapter 1

WEB OF LIES

"I cannot tell a lie."
George Washington

"The occasional exposure in the small print well after the fact will not prevent the regular stream of lies from setting the terms of debate and leaving the appropriate impressions firmly implemented."
Noam Chomsky

THE CONVENTIONAL WISDOM is that the decision to invade Iraq and topple Saddam Hussein was made long before the U.S. went to seek U.N. legitimacy. Some traced it back to 1992 when Paul Wolfowitz, after the Gulf War, co-authored with Lewis Libby, another political appointee at the Pentagon then, the Defence Planning Guidance. It envisioned the U.S. as an unrivalled ultra-power, "acting independently when collective action cannot be orchestrated." The Defence Planning Guidance was leaked to *The New York Times* in March 1992. It was subsequently watered down, but the spirit of this hyper-power idea seemed to have survived. The blueprint, indicative of the thinking of key officials of the Bush Administration, had appeared in other forms.

For instance, in September 2000 a think-tank headed by Dick Cheney, *Project for the New American Century*,[1] produced a report "Rebuilding America's Defenses". It said: "The United States has for decades sought to play a more permanent role in Gulf regional security. While the unresolved conflict with Iraq provides the immediate justification, the need for a substantial American military presence in the Gulf transcends the issue of the regime of Saddam Hussein." In 1998, *Project for the New American Century* wrote an angry letter to Bill Clinton for not removing Saddam Hussein. Nonetheless during Cheney's tenure at Halliburton, the company did $73 million worth of businesses with Saddam.[2]

In the wider scheme of things, Nine-eleven provided the justification to implement the thwarted mission. It wrapped up America with a sense of impunity and immunity. Two days after Nine-eleven, Paul Wolfowitz was already urging President George Bush to execute what many of the hawks had been longing for. Former NATO commander General Wesley Clark said he received calls on September 11 from "people around the White House urging him to link that assault to Saddam Hussein."

Seizing the moment, Ahmad Chalabi's[3] Iraq National Congress (INC) circulated a story on an Iraqi terrorist training camp at Salman Pak, where terrorists were supposedly taught how to hijack aeroplanes. Some of the front page "exclusives" published by American dailies on weapons of mass

---

1 The Washington hawks and neo-conservatives—Donald Rumsfeld, Paul Wolfowitz, Lewis Libby (Cheney's Chief of Staff) are members of Project for the New American Century formed in 1997.

2 Noor ad-Deen, "The Real Motives for War in Iraq", *IslamOnline*, Mar. 23, 2003

3 The Arabs taunt him as *Al-Hakim* (the thief).

destruction, a phrase created by Bush's aides, were actually written on the strength of information fed by the INC. This is a case of either the American intelligence tacitly allowing them to be misled or Ahmad Chalabi and company making a mockery of the American and also by extension British intelligence. Both countries were actively sharing information, leading Tony Blair to declare that the threat from Iraq was "serious and current". INC was funded by Pentagon, which, in turn, was relying on tips supplied by INC. At Pentagon, Paul Wolfowitz set up an Office of Special Plans headed by Abram Shulsky.[4] Veteran journalist Seymour Hersh wrote a series of brilliant articles on the American intelligence for *The New Yorker* in the lead up to the war. At that time, there were broad hints of the CIA being exasperated at the insistence of the war advocates for the intelligence services to corroborate their claims on the danger posed by Saddam Hussein. We can actually connect the dots. Testifying before the U.S. Senate Intelligence Committee in July 2003, CIA director George Tenet implied that the Office of Special Plans rewrote some of the intelligence on Iraq before passing it to the office of National Security Adviser Condoleeza Rice.[5]

---

4 Both Wolfowitz and Shulsky received their doctorates under political philosopher Leo Strauss at the University of Chicago in 1972. Strauss has many adherents. Others include William Kristol, editor of the Weekly Standard and Stephen Cambone, Under-Secretary of Defense for Intelligence. Critics of Straussian said they subscribe to a Plato idea that philosophers need to tell noble lies to the people at large and to powerful politicians. Read *The New Yorker* (May 12, 2003) "Selective Intelligence—Donald Rumsfeld has his own special sources. Are they reliable?"

5 Jason Leopold, "Tenet: Wolfowitz Did It The Yellowcake Blame Game", *Counterpunch*, July 19, 2003

Deputy National Security Adviser Stephen Hadley and another White House official acknowledged in July 2003 that there were two CIA memos dated October 5 and October 6 (2002), one addressed to Hadley and the other to speechwriter Michael Gerson. Both raised doubts about claims that Iraq was seeking uranium in Niger.

Despite the wishy-washy intelligence, war advocates on both sides of the Atlantic wasted little time in building a case against Iraq. I think bureaucrats and advisers assigned to pile up the arguments and facts knew precisely what was expected of them—to prove that Saddam Hussein posed an imminent threat. That, he had developed the most lethal weapon ever devised. An in-depth report by *The Washington Post* on the issue (August 10, 2003) said: "The new information indicates a pattern in which President Bush, Vice President Cheney and their subordinates—in public and behind the scenes—made allegations depicting Iraq's nuclear weapons program as more active, more certain and more imminent in its threat than the data they had would support. On occasion administration advocates withheld evidence that did not conform to their views. The White House seldom corrected misstatements or acknowledged loss of confidence in information upon which it had previously relied."

The attacks of September 11, 2001 had been disconcerting to the hyper-power that virtually anyone holding a grudge against the U.S. was a potential terrorist and hence must not be left unpunished. Under the circumstances, no agency dared to entertain differing views. No one wanted to be accused of being unpatriotic. Politicians harbouring doubts about the war were muted in their opposition for the same reason. This was when war advocates mixed spin and fact in their presentation.

Imagine the frenzy, and also the awkwardness. There must have been no new conclusive intelligence; how could there be any when the U.S. and Britain had comprehensively reined in on Saddam Hussein?

Donald Rumsfeld provided a confirmation of sorts on the deception when he said after the war: "We did not invade because we had discovered dramatic new evidence of Iraq's pursuit of weapons of mass murder ... we saw no new evidence in a new light through the prism of our experience in September 11."

The deaths and suffering of Iraqis as a result of the war preclude us from branding the whole episode as comical. It would have been as zany as the madness depicted in Evelyn Waugh's novel *Scoop* (1938) about excitable British war correspondents fomenting war in a far-flung country by wildly exaggerating the severity of a "political turmoil" as they jostled for news.

A torrent of euphemisms for lies and deceit ("misuse of intelligence" is an example) had been thrown in to sanitise the deception. That may not be able to prevent some high-profile resignations and casualties on both sides of the Atlantic. I sense that the half truths and deceptions over the past two years will be dredged out.

The world remembers that on October 7, 2002, President Bush hyped up the threat posed by Iraq in a stunning fashion. He said: "Iraq has trained al-Qaeda members in bomb making and poisons and deadly gasses .... (which) could allow the Iraqi regime to attack America without leaving any finger prints." Ironically it was the U.S. and Britain that were accusing Saddam of lies, deceptions and concealment. George Bush's presentation to the U.N. General Assembly on September 12, 2002 was called *A Decade of Lies and Deceit*. At about the same time, the London think-tank, the International Institute for Strategic Studies (IISS) produced a 78-page report that said the Iraqi nuclear weapons "could fall into the hands of terrorists." Secretly, preliminary planning for the war started in August 2002,[6] well before the U.S. said it was prepared to enforce regime change by military means.

In the meantime, accusations against Saddam were getting more acrobatic. Secretary of State Colin Powell told the U.N. on February 5, 2003:

> "Iraq today harbours deadly terrorist network headed by Abu Mussab al-Zarqawi, a collaborator of Osama bin Laden and his al-Qaeda lieutenants." Zarqawi did visit Baghdad but to seek medical treatment.

February 2003 saw the unveiling of the British's dodgy dossier, lifted from three articles on the Internet. By March 7, 2003 the alleged attempt by Iraq to "seek" uranium oxide from Niger for its nuclear programme had been debunked. The International Atomic Energy Agency (IAEA) said the document was forged. The war advocates were unfazed. Nine days later, Vice President Dick Cheney told NBC's Meet-the-Press on March 16, 2003: "We believe (Saddam) has, in fact, reconstituted nuclear weapons." Cheney repeated this astounding claim two days after the killing of Uday and Qusay. "No such thing" said Iraqi scientists interviewed after the war.

---

6 Peter Slevin and Dana Priest, "Wolfowitz Concedes Iraq Errors", *The Washington Post*, July 14, 2003

Also in March 2003, Tony Blair told *The Independent* newspaper that the U.N. had tried "unsuccessfully for 12 years to get Saddam to disarm peacefully". This came four years after a U.N. Security Council panel concluded: "a bulk of Iraq's proscribed weapons programmes has been eliminated." Tony Blair's earlier dossier presented to the House of Commons in September 2002 spoke of Iraq's attempt to import hardened aluminum tubes for gas centrifuges, used to enrich uranium for nuclear weapons. A 1999 British report admitted that it would take Iraq five years to enrich uranium. Two years later, the Americans confirmed this. In any case, Israel had destroyed Iraq's Osirak nuclear reactor in a 1981 air attack. Israel however has something like 200 nuclear warheads as at 1994 and has refused to sign any treaty regulating the use of nuclear weapons. On the contrary, between 1991 and 1998 the United Nations Special Commission (UNSCOM) identified and destroyed very large quantities of chemical weapons and ballistic missiles in Iraq. Until the U.S. and Britain comprehensively explain all the paradoxes and ambiguities, suspicions will deepen. The old trick of branding "dissenters", those who dare to question the ways of the superpower, as "rogues", "prickly", "discredited" or "conspiracy theorists" may not work this time.

Indeed, months had lapsed after the fall of Saddam; a 1,600-strong team combing Iraq to search for dangerous weapons has yielded nothing. It has been suggested that Saddam could have destroyed the weapons. This was exactly what the international community wanted him to do to avert invasion. He should be congratulated, not ousted.

Before the war, we were told about those 650km-range missiles that could hit Israel and British troops stationed in Cyprus. The "awesome" arsenal of Iraq included 25,000 litres of anthrax, 500 tonnes of Sarin, mustard gas and VV nerve agent. This was the American president in his State of the Union address. Blair had two days before war began, told the House of Commons Iraq had far reaching plans to weaponise VX.

Were Bush and Blair merely talking up the threat or this was a premeditated design? Bush said Iraq had 30,000 munitions capable of delivering chemical weapons plus several weapons laboratories and an active nuclear weapons development programme. The truth is the U.N. inspectors had not found any nuclear, chemical or biological weapons in Iraq since at least 1994. This was well known in the intelligence circles. Those poisonous gases produced using the Iraqi method must be used fast, within one to eight weeks.

Curiously, Paul Wolfowitz told *Vanity Fair* the focus on Iraq's WMD was done on "bureaucratic reasons ... because it was the one reason everyone could agree upon." He has been changing his mind. He later said the intelligence on WMD "is murky".

None of the hawks or neo-conservatives have owned up to the fallacies. This is a strategic move. Rumsfeld appeared to have dramatically cut down on his public comments. Others including Cheney have been dishing out excuses and glib talk. It came as no surprise to me that the right-wingers had leapt to the defence of the Bush Administration. William Kristol, editor of *The Weekly Standard*, wrote in *The Washington Post* that the Niger blunder was "probably a mistake, (but) didn't change anything."

In fact, retired diplomat Joseph Wilson who exposed the Niger ruse having been assigned by Washington to check on the veracity of Iraq's plan to seek uranium supplies, was hounded. He told NBC News on July 21, 2003 that the White House deliberately leaked his wife's identity as a covert CIA operative. We now wonder the extent of such covert CIA operatives. Now that the failure of American intelligence is a major issue, perhaps more such operatives will be signed up, including those in the very organisations being spied upon. This, according to retired senior intelligence officers who wrote to *The Economist* in July 2003, was a crucial link in the intelligence network.

The failure of intelligence has dire consequences as Nine-eleven signified. In Iraq, the issue was not the failure of intelligence, but the use and embellishment of suspect intelligence. The fact of the matter is the accusers of Saddam had exaggerated the urgency of it, talked up suspicions and presented possibility as a fact.

John Kerry, a Democrat presidential hopeful who actually served in Vietnam said if Bush had lied "he had lied to me personally".

This has not prevented Bush from declaring on July 14, 2003 that Saddam Hussein 'absolutely' had weapons programmes. Bush said: "And we gave him a chance to let the inspectors in, but he would not let them in."

Blair, on his part, is peddling the moral reason, saying that even if the WMD would not be found "a menace had been defeated." He told the U.S. Congress in July 2003: "If we are wrong (about WMD), we will have destroyed a threat that at the very least is responsible for inhuman carnage and suffering. That is something I am confident history will forgive." On the same day, Bush said: "As long as I hold this office, I will never risk the lives of American citizens by assuming the goodwill of dangerous enemies." Such coordinated response by Washington and London has been a constant feature since the war on terror started. Both offices are conscious of presentation. The presentation turned out to be suspiciously flawed and misleading.

Bush, playing the role of the courageous commander-in-chief, used to think, miraculously, that evidence can be found linking Saddam to al-Qaeda. Bush has since tampered his self-assuredness when he said: "But it's going to take time to gather the evidence and analyse the mounds ... the miles of documents we have uncovered." Jay Bookman, who is the deputy editorial page editor of the *Atlanta Journal-Constitution*, said the official story on Iraq "has never made sense".

I just hope that the "evidence" to be presented is actual weapons that kill, not programmes and plans to acquire such weapons—dreaming of owning something is not a crime. Certainly no justification for a full-scale invasion and occupation.

Chapter 2

U.S. LOST THE ARGUMENT

"All truth passes through three stages. First, it is ridiculed. Second, it is violently opposed. Third, it is accepted as being self-evident."

Arthur Schopenhauer

MANY international commentators were undeniably ambivalent about the Saddam Hussein's regime—who should decide if it was nasty and should be changed? Under normal circumstances, such things are best left to voters. Elections conducted by Saddam, however, had eerily produced near-unanimous outcomes to serve as a reliable guide, a gauge of feelings and a means of change.

Then again the qualities of Saddam's Government were never really the issue. Morality, the popularity and competency of the Government do not normally trigger wars.

Wars are messy, never clean and precise. The worry now is how much more suffering and despair will Iraqis have to brave before normalcy is restored. Basic decisions about the lives of Iraqis are out of their hands. This regime change has been forced upon Iraqis. The much-vaunted democratic ideals espoused by the U.S. and Britain have been betrayed by such appalling lapses as the manner justice is being meted out on the "unlawful combatants" being held in Guantánamo Bay, Cuba. On this fundamental issue, the British opposed the cryptic trials by military tribunals that the U.S. wanted. The U.S. has since made limited concessions.

While the reasons to go to war in Iraq have been pretty much ambiguous, the arguments put forward by the critics of U.S. and Britain have been unfailingly credible.

One, Saddam was previously accommodated and assisted by the twin occupiers of Iraq, the U.S. and Britain. Second, as the world sole superpower, the U.S. has an undisguised vested interest in the Middle East. It guzzles lots of oil and the region produces lots of oil. Third, the U.S. is unapologetically the chief backer of an Israel smacked in a sea of Arabs. Does America care greatly what the rest of the world thinks of it?

I have my doubts.

Because, the might of the super power drives many players to, in the end, cosy up to the Americans. That does not mean the rest of the world warmly accepts the American hegemony, let alone to allow a few strong-willed advisers reorder the world. Already there are inconsistencies about the conduct of the Americans and the Britons even as they straddle the world telling others how to behave.

The British Scott Enquiry into the arms-to-Iraq affair revealed that the British Government secretly supplied Saddam with "more weapons-related equipment even after he shelled the Kurdish town of Halabja in March 1988 with gas bombs, killing an estimated 5,000 civilians and maiming thousands more."[1]

The U.S. chipped in with vital intelligence, military advice, and according to declassified documents, Washington had authorised the sale of poisonous chemical and biological viruses such as anthrax to Baghdad. In 1983, Donald Rumsfeld who is the present-day U.S. Defense Secretary, had traveled to Baghdad as a special presidential envoy to meet Saddam. His mission was to normalise Washington-Baghdad ties "at a time when Iraq was using chemical weapons on an almost daily basis".[2]

Saddam's fortune changed after his monumental error of judgment in dispatching his forces to Kuwait in 1990, although curiously the American Ambassador left Baghdad a week before the invasion. Innocent Iraqis paid a heavy price. Crippling sanctions claimed the lives of 1.7 million Iraqis. On paper, Iraq should be rich. It is blessed with the second largest oil reserves in the world, but the sanctions robbed the country of some $150 billion in forfeited oil revenues. Not only Saddam's military was crushed, America and Britain hanged around, hounding him. Saddam's tormentors created two No Fly Zones that meant the remaining 200 or so Iraqi military planes could not go out there without the risk of being gunned down. Given such inactivity, and with the air superiority of the U.S., Iraqi air force or whatever left of it, would be overwhelmed in a flash in the event of a war. To make sure the Iraqi air force would not show up in the actual "showdown", between June 2002 and the start of the inva-

---

1 Richard-Norton-Taylor, "Don't Trust Bush or Blair on Iraq", *The Guardian*, Aug. 21, 2002

2 Michael Dobbs, "U.S. Had a Key Role in Iraq Build-up", *The Washington Post*, Dec. 30, 2002

sion on March 19, 2003, the U.S. flew 21,736 sorties over Southern Iraq. 371 targets were attacked. This was the military doctrine preferred by Rumsfeld; to impair the enemy's ability to fight. Hence, nine months before war commenced, five months before Resolution 1441 was passed, U.S. planes were systematically destroying remnants of the Iraqi air defences and communications grids in preparations for a land war. I remember Saddam's regime cataloguing the air strikes then, but the world was no longer listening.

The sneering world started looking at Iraq with a mixture of fear and irritation after the tragic occupation of Kuwait. The U.N. dispatched a U.S.-led military force to liberate Kuwait. This was achieved swiftly. But the U.N. mandate did not cover the ouster of the Saddam regime, so the troops went home. Saddam picked up the pieces. Iraq's restless Shia[3] majority launched an uprising in Basra in the South but minus the U.S.-led military might, Saddam crushed them. The Kurds in the North had the U.N. protection in the form of a No Fly Zone. The composition of Iraq had always been combustible—20 per cent Sunnah, 20 per cent Kurds and 60 per cent Shias.

Saddam rose to power in 1979. That year, there was a revolution in neighbouring Iran. An Islamic Republic had replaced a monarchy. The Ayatollah who became supreme leader of Iran, had for 14 years previously lived in exile in the Iraq's Shia town of Najaf. In 1978, Baghdad asked Ayatollah Khomeini to leave at the behest of the Shah of Iran. In 1980, Saddam attacked Iran. Ten years later after a war of attrition with Iran, Saddam invaded a smaller but richer neighbour

---

3 The Shias are also referred to as 'Shites' and the Sunnah Muslims as 'Sunni'.

Kuwait, ostensibly, for Kuwait's refusal to foot part of the bill to wage war on Iran.

There was never a country called Iraq until 1920. This was the root-cause of all the travails of Iraq. The Ottoman Empire was breaking up. The British and French agreed to carve out remnants of the Empire into their protectorates. Baghdad and two other Ottoman provinces, Basra and Mosul were assigned to the British. The then Colonial Secretary Winston Churchill decided to put together a country by merging the three provinces. Churchill served briefly as Colonial Secretary when he did not have a good grasp on the Arab World. He relied on T.E. Lawrence, the British military officer who fought alongside the Arabs during the Arab Revolt.

In 1921, the British gave Iraq a King. Feisal was the son of Sherif Hussein of Mecca and a confidante of Lawrence. Leaders of the Arab Revolt were not bent on removing the Turks, said many historical accounts, neither were they excited about the British. There were however promises and opportunities; so they fought. After the war, the British sent Feisal to be King of Syria, another new country. But the French had been promised Syria, so they brought down the King. State-less, the British asked him to go to Baghdad instead. Abdullah, a brother of Feisal was given TransJordan apparently on the grounds that he was not expected to resist the Zionists planning a country next door. In the meantime, the British ruled Iraq through its mandate. The mandate ended in 1932. The Iraqi Government carried out a massacre of the Nestorian Christians who had been closely associated with the Mandate Government. Some Western historians had since argued that despite creating new Arab States unilaterally and at such speed, Churchill had been vindicated.

These historians point to the "success" of Jordan as a State even though it was created to pacify Abdullah.

I say the British bore responsibility for the fragility and rancorous ethnic relations that had dogged Iraq. In creating the new States, the British ignored the feelings and preferences of local Arabs. The Arabs were bullied into co-existing with others.

Arabs are diverse. Eric Rouleau, a former French ambassador to Tunisia and Turkey observed: "On a personal level, an Egyptian Muslim would feel closer to a Christian Copt than, say, a citizen of Saudi Arabia or Morocco. Palestinian refugees were not integrated in 'brotherly countries' not only because they were perceived as aliens, but also because they would not and could not assimilate with people harbouring them." Yet after the breakup of the Ottoman Empire, the West neglected the Kurds who didn't get a country. To this day, they still habour hopes of independence.

Iraq was such a haphazard creation. But, really, it was the U.N. sanctions in the wake of the liberation of Kuwait that thoroughly crippled and stifled Iraq.

The sinister crumbling of Iraq as a result of the sanctions took place during the Clinton Administration. Clinton resisted calls including from key members of the present Bush's Republican Government to force out Saddam Hussein. The Bush Administration brought together a number of likeminded neo-conservatives, many of whom staunch backers of the Likud Party of Israel. Some of the neo-conservatives happened to be stridently anti-Soviet during the Cold War. The end of the Cold War compelled these strategists and intellectuals to look for a new cause. Many turned to the Middle East.

It is in part for this reason that we detect a clear shift in the focal point after the Cold War. Throughout 1980s, the Central America supplied much of the world headlines. Then, in a flash, the likes of Nicaragua, Costa Rica and Panama ceased to be troubled spots. As if someone had brandished the magic wand. In the Middle East, America's dual-containment policy that was applied to Iran and Iraq was modified. Iraq became an immediate priority. Libya's "indiscretions" retreated to the footnotes.

Enter Paul Wolfowitz who used to feature in the Pacific Dialogue hosted jointly by Malaysian think-tanks in the 1990s and who had served in various capacities in Washington. During the Clinton Administration, Wolfowitz was among those urging the White House to topple Saddam.

After Nine-eleven, Wolfowitz renewed his call at a meeting of the President George Bush's inner circle. While the idea quickly caught on, the Bush Administration vacillated badly on how to justify the action.

Judging by the incoherent arguments they had put forward since, massaging public opinion at the international level did not seem to matter terribly to the war planners.

It seems to me that they saw in Nine-eleven a long-awaited impetus, an excuse even, that could conceivably legitimise military actions that would otherwise be divisive. The scorned hyper-power is entitled to retaliate indiscriminately, so seemed to be the thinking. As President Bush said in a prime time news conference in March 2003: "When it comes to our security, we really don't need anybody's permission."

The groundwork for invasion started much earlier. We can trace it back to Bush's State of the Union address on

January 29, 2002, when he explicitly broadened the war-on-terror intent to also "prevent the terrorists and regimes that seek chemical, biological, or nuclear weapons from threatening the United States and the world." This was the Axis of Evil speech; it became palpable at this juncture that Iraq would be next after Afghanistan.

The al-Qaeda link was however proving hard to reinforce. The Bush Administration began by accusing Saddam of harbouring remnants of al-Qaeda in the wake of the Afghan War. This was a reference to Ansar al-Islam group that did receive some mentions during the actual Iraq War. Among them, 150 battle-weary Arabs fleeing Afghanistan; the Kurds who controlled Northern Iraq arrested 15 to 20 of these fighters. Much to their dismay, U.S. officials were not interested to talk to them.

Also dropped precipitously was a phony claim that Egyptian Mohammad Atta, a suspected ringleader in the World Trade Center attacks, had met with an Iraqi spy in Prague in April 2001. Paul Wolfowitz tried hard to frame evidence. CIA too failed to connect. When Wolfowitz persisted, the then Czech Republic President Vaclav Havel reportedly had to telephone President Bush for the claim to be dropped. No such meeting ever took place.

After a lull, Donald Rumsfeld[4] and National Security Adviser Condoleeza Rice[5] revived the link in September 2002. They were possibly unnerved by the kind of reports being published by *The Washington Post* then. The newspaper said: "... the CIA has yet to find convincing evidence despite hav-

4 "Rumsfeld seeks to connect Iraq with al-Qaeda", *Financial Times*, Sept. 26, 2002

5 "Rice: Iraq Shelters, Arms al Qaeda", *Associated Press*, Sept. 25, 2002

ing combed its files and redoubled its efforts to collect and analyze information related to Iraq."[6]

CIA was not convinced there was such a link. This led Rumsfeld and Wolfowitz to set up the alternative intelligence-gathering unit, in part, to show a link between Saddam's regime and al-Qaeda. Dick Cheney, on his part, made multiple trips to CIA to meet with Iraq analysts.[7]

Former National Security Adviser Brent Scowcroft offered some wisdom amidst the hysteria-like reactions. "Suppose there had been no Nine-eleven attack. Saddam Hussein would still be doing exactly what he is doing. He is not a problem for us because of terrorism."

Throughout year 2002, we were warned Saddam could pass the deadly weapons to terrorist groups, al-Qaeda included. Iraq's Tariq Aziz protested: "The whole world knows we are ideologically different." Indeed Iraq and al-Qaeda are natural enemies. According to Daniel Benjamin, who co-authored *The Age of Sacred Terror*, "a central tenet of al-Qaeda's jihadis ideology is that secular Muslim rulers and their regimes have oppressed the believers and plunged Islam into a historic crisis."[8] Unfazed, Rumsfeld promised that the Bush Administration had "bulletproof evidence" of al-Qaeda-Iraq link, and Powell made a similar case to the U.N. A year later, the two highest-ranking al-Qaeda operatives in custody—Khalid Shekih Mohamd and Abu Zubaydah, told investigators that Osama shunned cooperation with Saddam Hussein.

---

6 "U.S. Not Claiming Iraqi Link to Terror", *The Washington Post*, Sept. 10, 2002

7 *The Washington Post*, June 5, 2003

8 Daniel Benjamin, "Saddam Hussein and al-Qaeda Are Not Allies", *New York Times*, Sept. 30, 2002

Daniel Benjamin who has always doubted that Saddam would ever pass weapons of mass destruction "to terrorists who might use it against you" again argued in *The New York Times* on July 21, 2003 that the secularists of Baathist Iraq and al-Qaeda "simply do not trust each other".

The truth was while Iraq did throw Palestine into the equation during the 1991 Gulf War, it had earlier thrown out Palestinian fighters.

Baghdad had in 1978 closed the Al Fatah offices, seized arms on transit and evicted the likes of George Habash's Popular Front for the Liberation of Palestine and Abu Nidal's Fatah Revolutionary Council.[9]

Abu Nidal was indeed found dead in Baghdad in August 2002. But according to U.S. State Department report, Abu Nidal had long retired. The report said Abu Nidal "had not attacked Western targets since the late 1980s."

By July-August 2003 as the WMD fiasco exploded on both sides of the Atlantic, scrutiny has also turned to false allegations linking Saddam's Iraq to al-Qaeda. In an August 2003 speech highly critical of the war, former Vice President Al Gore said: "Enormous numbers of Americans thus came to believe that Saddam Hussein was involved in the September 11 attacks and was actively supporting al-Qaeda."

Many had expected pressure to mount on the likes of Wolfowitz and Rumsfeld, but the scrutiny has hardly troubled them. During a spell, Wolfowitz was the point man, appearing on television interviews to justify the invasion. Yet the more visible he was, the more flaws in his arguments

---

9 Count de Marenches and David A. Andelmen, *The Fourth World War: Diplomacy and Espionage in the Age of Terrorism*, William Morrow, New York, 1992

were detected. He said one thing in the *Vanity Fair* interview in May 2003, the transcript of which was released by Pentagon. Then, iced-cool, he will appear on NBC's Meet-the-Press programme to try and improve his spin. By accentuating this pattern, I am not suggesting that Wolfowitz is being prepared as Bush Administration's fall guy if things go from bad to worse. He is the leading intellectual in the Administration with impeccable credentials, and the most influential No. 2 in a long while. Still, if the ratings slide further, and elections inch closer, and an important personality has to be sacrificed, there is no better candidate than the one identified closely with the Iraqi invasion. The controversy engulfing Tony Blair over the death of Government scientist Dr. David Kelly provided respite to Wolfowitz, Cheney and Rumsfeld. Then again, Bush may promote Wolfowitz.

Earlier, such conundrum was furthest from the mind of Bush's speechwriters when they decided to re-insert the alleged Iraq-al-Qaeda links into another of President Bush's State of the Union address, on January 28, 2003. This was the same speech that controversially included Saddam's alleged attempt to get uranium from Africa. Later in a July 2003 African visit, Bush said he had read it because the contents had been cleared by the CIA.

Continuing the pattern of synchronised spin[10] between London and Washington, on the same day (January 28, 2003) Tony Blair told the House of Commons there was such a link but he could not exactly say how they were an item. This was a day after the two U.N. weapons inspectors reported that there had been no evidence that Iraq had re-

10 Some British politicians believe the word "spin" in itself is a spin. They say the proper word for "spin" is "manipulation".

vived its nuclear weapons despite new information provided by Washington and London.

By then the WMD claims had been amplified; curiously we were routinely advised to be pessimistic about the work of the U.N. inspectors. Tony Blair wrote on December 16, 2002: "The weapons inspectors are at work. Because of Saddam Hussein's record of lies, concealment ..., one must be skeptical that he will willingly give up his weapons of mass destruction."

That the West was determined to invade Iraq was a badly kept secret. Laughably, however, the most incriminating evidence unearthed by January 2003 had been the discovery of "11 empty, 22-mm warheads designed to carry chemical weapons". In case everyone recovered their senses and saw through the propaganda machine, we were warned against trusting the Iraqis who have been manufacturing a "programme of lies and deception".

The U.S. and Britain kept telling the world "time is running out for Iraq". Paradoxically, they also burnished the contention that Baghdad was not going to give full cooperation. They insisted that the onus was on Iraq to tell the world what had happened to the 30,000 chemical weapons it allegedly used to have. In response, Iraq quoted Bill Clinton who had since told the Labour Party Conference that the weapons inspectors destroyed more weapons in Iraqi possession than the Gulf War ever did. Long before Mohamed El Baradei became a world celebrity, the head of the International Atomic Energy Agency had vouched that Baghdad's nuclear programmes had been neutralised when weapons inspectors left in 1998.

Strategic Interests

The U.S. did turn to the U.N., lured by the attractive bonus of winning the international body's backing to wage war on Iraq. It secured U.N. Security Council's approval for Resolution 1441 on November 8, 2002 after two months of negotiations.

This episode aptly demonstrated that countries still single-mindedly and vigorously pursue their strategic interests, despite all the rhetoric on borderless world spun the last two decades. Russian oil companies had been particularly anxious. France had been doing business in Iraq for decades. In fact, Iraq reportedly retaliated to the Russian vote by scrapping the deal with Russia's Lukoil in the development of its key West Qurna oil field.[11] The Qurna deal signed in 1997 was a $20 billion contract. "Such a deal could evaporate along with the Saddam regime, along with the Russian giant Zarubezneft, which was granted a potential $90 billion concession to develop the bin Umar oil field," *The Observer* said.

China, in the run-up to the vote, was as calculative. *The Guardian* East Asian Editor, John Gittings noticed that China did not publicly criticise the U.S.-British draft resolutions, leaving the business of dissension to France and Russia. China was pleased that the U.S. had removed a major irritant for it, in the form of nagging criticisms of its human rights abuses in the Xinjiang region.

"Washington has already made a downpayment by listing the Eastern Turkestan Islamic Movement as a terrorist or-

---

11 "Russia attacks Iraq over Lukoil", *Financial Times*, Dec. 16, 2002

ganisation,"[12] wrote Gittings, before the vote. East Turkestan was the name of two short-lived independent Uighur republics, established in 1933 and 1944. Like many other Governments facing Muslim independent movements, China tried to link the Uighurs with al-Qaeda. The war on terrorism became an instant mockery.

What Resolution 1441 had sought to achieve?

This hinges on whom you talked to. Beguilingly, John Negroponte, the U.S. Ambassador to the U.N., said after the two U.N. weapons inspector chiefs briefed the U.N. Security Council on January 27, 2003, that all the Resolution had sought to achieve were:

- Whether Iraq will submit accurate reports on WMD
- Whether it would cooperate unconditionally.

The U.S., ominously, seemed indifferent to the question of WMD; the Americans were hinting broadly that the U.N. could not disarm Iraq anyway. The ambiguities have after the official war in Iraq ended, returned to haunt both Washington and London.

"Where is the threat?" Yahya Mahmassani, Arab League Representative to U.N. had asked in an interview with the BBC then. This is "double standards", he bellowed.

Double standards because America had either vetoed or abstained in Security Council Resolutions on Israel on too many occasions. The Jewish State gets $3 billion in annual U.S. aid even as most Palestinians live in poverty. The

---

12 John Gittings, "Hidden Dangers", *The Guardian*, Oct. 25, 2002

"Symington Accord"[13] prevents the U.S. Government from granting aid to countries that develop nuclear weapons outside the international control and agreement". In 1994, *Jane's Intelligence Review*, the world authority on the arms industry, confirmed that Israel has 200 nuclear warheads, making it the world's sixth largest nuclear power. When the BBC exposed this in July 2003, the British public broadcaster was branded "anti-Semitic".

Intriguingly despite the U.S.'s purported fears for Iraq's WMD, it emerged in the run-up to Iraq War,[14] the "Pentagon is developing a new generation of weapons that undermine and possibly violate international treaties on biological and chemical warfare". *The Guardian* revealed that in the pipeline were big plans—"non-lethal" weapons similar to the narcotic gas used by Russian forces to tragically end a recent hostage drama at a Moscow theatre, included.

Since the U.S. embarked on the campaign against Iraq, more instances of double standards had surfaced; the latest concerned North Korea's nuclear power. Henry Kissinger was among those who believed North Korea posed a bigger threat to the U.S. than Saddam Hussein. America might be influenced by the spectre of body bags in using the soft-approach on North Korea. If war breaks out in the Korean Peninsula, the casualties could be as high as one million, including 100,000 Americans.

---

13 Hilary Wainwright, "Israel's arms inspector", *The Guardian*, Oct. 4, 2002

14 Julian Borger, "U.S. weapons secrets exposed", *The Guardian*, Oct. 29, 2002

Muslims were further annoyed by the outlandish arguments coming out of America to try and justify America's overflowing compassion for the North Koreans.

New York Times columnist William Safire argued: "Saddam Hussein is a recent, serial aggressor, while totalitarian North Korea has not launched an invasion in the past half-century. Moreover the potentially high human cost of wiping out the Korean threat should be an unforgettable lesson to every nation. The world must not allow Iraq to gain the level of destructive power that appeasement and misplaced trust permitted North Korea to achieve."

I should thus venture to ask: Might this then encourage rogue states to build nuclear programmes precipitously to escape the dragnet? The fact of the matter is North Korea does not have oil or Israel as a neighbour.

As they prepared to invade Iraq, the U.S. and Britain hyped up the fruits of reconstruction and democracy, prompting Robert Fisk of *The Independent* to catalogue major past promises to the Muslim world.

- 1915: T.E. Lawrence promises Arab independence in the return for the support of such leaders as Sherif Hussein of Mecca;
- 1944: President Roosevelt assures King Ibn Saud that U.S. will not allow the Palestinians to be dispossessed;
- 1979-90: Presidents Carter and Reagan promise to help rebuild Afghanistan if the *mujahideen* expels the Soviet army;
- 1991: George Bush promises an "oasis of peace" in the Middle East in return for Arab support in the Gulf War;

- 2001: Tony Blair assures Yasser Arafat of Britain's commitment to "viable Palestinian state", including Jerusalem.

Propagandists additionally invoked the Japanese experience; so General Tommy Franks would have been the Iraqi MacArthur. "Contrary to what self-anointed 'realists' seem to be suggesting today," wrote John Dower, "most of the factors that contributed to the success of nation-building in occupied Japan would be absent in an Iraq military defeated by the United States."[15]

Douglas MacArthur walked into a Japan hated by the whole of Asia for the despair it wrought. Emperor Hirohito endorsed the conquerors and the Japanese "quickly blamed their own militaristic leaders for having initiated a miserable, unwinnable war." They went about picking up the pieces hardly troubling the U.S. Military Administration throughout their seven-year rule.

Yes, Germany and Japan, were occupied and reconstructed after World War II, but they were the aggressors. Iraq was not going to attack anyone. Iraq was not in a position to do so even if it so desired. "Iraq is no Japan," said Saudi Foreign Minister Prince Saud Al-Faisal in an interview with CNN on November 3, 2002.

As 2002 drew to a close, international public opinion was ranged against the U.S.; the resistance was bigger than what Vietnam saw. I was in London when 1.5 million souls poured to the streets to protest the war. I joined them.

---

[15] John Dower, "Lessons From Japan About War's Aftermath", *New York Times*, Oct. 27, 2002

Such outpouring of emotions compelled the U.S. to fight a relentless propaganda war. There was this leaked plan to prosecute Saddam, his two sons Uday and Qusay, Ali Hassan al-Majeed, known as "Chemical Ali" for his alleged use of chemical weapons against the Kurds in northern Iraq, and Izzat Ibrahim, vice chairman of Iraq's Revolutionary Command Council.[16]

Militarily, and this was unknown to the outside world, the U.S. was being assuaged by mounting evidence that Iraqi resistance would be meek. Experts told U.S. Senate foreign relations committee that at least half of the Iraqi regular Army was at 70 per cent or less of its authorised strength, with some infantry units severely undermanned.[17] Under the circumstances, the conventional wisdom was Saddam would lure the U.S. into an urban warfare to pile up the American body bags that numbered 300-odd in the Gulf War, increase the civilian casualties and hence earn international sympathy.

In the end, Saddam's defences crumbled overnight. Until then, the likelihood of the American military being bogged and hunted down in an urban warfare had exercised and alarmed the Generals. It emerged as a source of discord between them and the Pentagon hawks. A *New York Times* report on August 11, 2003 said that the U.S. military and the CIA started operating in Iraq three months before the war started.

The newspaper report said: "Iraqis and officials from other Arab countries who were involved in the advance operation in Iraq said American contacts with Iraqi officers had

16 Peter Slevin, "U.S. Seeks War Crimes Trial Data", *The Washington Post*, Oct. 30, 2002

17 "Loyalty of Iraq's elite in doubt", *The Guardian*, Sept. 20, 2002

been arranged beginning in late 2002 by Jordanian intelligence officers who were working with U.S. Special Forces and CIA agents.

"They said the operation was led by military's Task Force 20 and that the contacts included telephone calls, e-mail messages, visits and in some cases the payment of substantial sums of money.

"The efforts to court Iraqi commanders, and the subsequent dissolution of the Iraqi Army, offers a partial explanation—along with the sheer brutality of the bombardment that the Iraqi Army suffered—for the light resistance that the advancing Americans often faced."

Post-Saddam Iraq

First Iran and then Syria; the war on Iraq was reportedly engineered to turn the whole of Arab and Muslim world into a democracy, supposedly, pro-Western. That's the grand vision of the hawks or neo-conservatives.

Indeed, Nine-eleven had stirred the neo-conservatives and the unilateralists in Washington. They were the "war party", those who think ousting Saddam "would precipitate a cascade of democratisation throughout the Arab and Muslim world, beginning with Iran and Syria but eventually encompassing Egypt, Saudi and a future Palestinian state."[18]

Iraq was an opportunity to add the glamorous term "Doctrine" to Bush's name, as several past presidents had—Carter Doctrine, Reagan Doctrine, Monroe Doctrine, and Roosevelt Doctrine. The Bush Doctrine allows America to

---

18 David Remnick and Hendrik Hertzberg, Comment, "A Year After", *The New Yorker*, Sept. 16, 2002

have a go at other countries or groups if it says that the target is potentially dangerous in the form of pre-emptive strikes. Many think it reeks of haughty American Imperialism and I say they are spot on.

It reminds us of American misdeeds, like CIA's covert operation to overthrow the Iranian Government of Prime Minister Dr. Mohamed Mossadegh in 1953. Details of the operation are available on *The New York Times* website "The C.I.A in Iran—Secrets of History".

A year later, the democratically elected President of Guatemala suffered the same fate when he tried to "apply agrarian land reform laws to idle land owned by United Fruit Company". Opponents saw that as a move to nationalise the plantations. The company had powerful backers in Washington.[19]

By accident, Nine-eleven too, was preceded in history by another September 11, a military takeover in Chile in 1973 that toppled the elected President Salvador Allende, and installed General Augusto Pinochet. Pinochet has since been reviled internationally. This was not so in 1973 at least in the eyes of the U.S. Pinochet and the Junta quickly "banned political parties, put Congress on indefinite recess, instituted Press censorship, jailed opponents and cancelled elections" as the CIA worked to polish the Junta's image at home and abroad.[20]

---

19 From an article by the Mexican writer Carlos Fuentes that first appeared in *El Pais International* (Madrid).

20 From the National Security Archive website: Chile and the United States: Declassified Documents Relating to the military coup, Sept. 11, 1973.

There were also attempts to assassinate Fidel Castro and Muammar Gaddafi and in 2002, a White House spokesman, no less, said "if a bullet for Saddam Hussein could do the trick, why not?"

The Religious Factor

For all its rhetoric, America has not been pursuing a strictly ethical foreign policy. This fallacy has not shown signs of waning under the Bush Doctrine. And what's more is that systematically the war on terror quickly took on graver dimensions, like developing into a religious clash. Overnight, age-old conflicts involving Muslims in Kashmir, Chechnya and Palestine acquired a new branding—terrorism, their Governments bolstered by the Americans' tacit backing. Intellectuals writing for the op-ed (opinion and editorial) pages of the leading dailies tirelessly spotlighted the myths. The Bush Administration was blissfully oblivious of the very public opinion it was supposed to try to influence.

George Bush who like Tony Blair is Bible-reading, refrained from criticising his Christian Right backers who tore into Islam, prompting American editorials to compare his silence to his earlier utterances to rally support for the strike on Afghanistan. Chairman of the U.S. House of Representatives Sub-Committee on Terrorism and Homeland Security, Rep. C. Saxby Chambliss (R-Georgia) reportedly told Georgia state law enforcement officials that they should "just turn (the sheriff) loose and have him arrest every Muslim that crosses the state line."

The U.S. now requires visitors from some Muslim countries to register personally with the INS. They risk detention and deportation if they don't do just that. Denials that this was racial profiling sounded feeble. The U.S. Patriot Act gives unlimited powers to spy on citizens, and Arab Americans are worried.

Chapter 3

RENEWED ARAB PARALYSIS

"Cowards can never be moral."
Mahatma Gandhi

WASHINGTON AND LONDON stridently ignored the deafening protests over the imminent attack on Iraq. More strictures were issued and troops mobilised to the Middle East even as Hans Blix, the now retired U.N. chief weapons inspector, and colleagues had not concluded their job; even as the U.S. and Britain were twisting arms, Africans mainly, to secure a second U.N. Resolution that would have authorised war. The troop deployment was, according to the spin doctors, a means of avoiding war. Nobody believed them.

The world was clamouring for hard evidence. This was in vain. In January 2003, Tony Blair faced down scowling British who asked if he realised that going to war without a second U.N. resolution would "split Britain down the middle".[1] The British Prime Minister upped the ante on Saddam's link to terrorists. Blair stupendously claimed that a terrorist attack on Britain was "inevitable" thus justifying unilateral aggression on Iraq.

The ever-bellicose American rhetoric further vilified Saddam Hussein. The dangerously ill-defined term "radical Islam" was being waved in the West as big a threat as Soviet Communism was. They destroyed Soviet Communism once Mikhail Gorbachev entertained doubts about Soviet Communism's viability without reforms, doubts precipitated by the debacle over Afghanistan. Ironically, North Korea was coaxed, cajoled and caressed for possessing nuclear capability. An Arab cartoonist had Kim Jong Il of North Korea catapulting a missile toward the U.S.; likening the perilous caper to "*Intifada*—Of the Heavy Kind ..."

Some of the questions that were troubling me endlessly were leaping to the fore: Is the Arab-Muslim World under siege? Are the Muslims being singled out as the new international pariah, the world savage requiring to be tamed, emasculated and converted? Is democracy and human rights so alien to Arab and Muslim societies? Was Islam not a message of emancipation, enlightenment, empowerment and human rights long before the European West woke up to these ideals?

Democracy is not new to Arabs. Prophet Muhammad introduced the system in Medina long before the West thought about human rights and empowerment. Now overnight Muslims are the enemy? Why so?

---

1 BBC World showed live Blair's meeting with a Commons committee on Iraq, Jan. 21, 2003

Crown Prince Abdullah of Saudi Arabia offered his analysis: "We are targeted. The aim is not any country but the Islamic faith, but Islam will remain strong with the support of God and its followers."[2]

The Arabs did work hard to avert war by crafting, not very discreetly, a possible exile for Saddam or as *Time* magazine reported—by "encouraging Iraqi generals to overthrow Saddam and his inner circle."

As a Muslim non-Arab observer, I watched events in the post-Resolution 1441 with trepidation. The whole business of getting a U.N. Resolution and sending in weapons inspectors was to disarm Iraq, not to interfere with Iraqi domestic affairs. But the spirit of 1441 was quickly wrecked.

I asked myself then: Are the Arabs confused or are they following Bush blindly? Preparing for war, the U.S. strutted about; their self-esteem soared. They knew the Arabs would just fall in line. On February 15, 2003, some eight million protest marchers poured onto the streets worldwide—3 million in Europe, 2 million in Spain and 1.5 million in London. Arab Street protests were faint, heard only in Syria and Morocco. I wonder if the West would have dared invade Iraq if the Arabs holler their protests and oppositions, and dispatch tens of thousands of Arab volunteer peace protesters to Iraq?

Instead it was the peace movements of the West who were sending volunteers to Baghdad, to protest invasion and war. If the Arabs could get a few thousands European/Americans to go to Baghdad as human shields, many were convinced that the attack on Baghdad would have been reconsidered. The British government was reported to have said it

2 "Prince Abdullah sees no war on Iraq", *Arab News*, Jan. 13, 2003

would reconsider an attack if 1,000 British citizens were to go to Baghdad as human shields. It proves that Arab lives have less value. It demonstrates how much contempt they have for the Arabs.

This is also developing into a war of ironies—the world's biggest exporter of democracy, the U.S. has imposed fines on a number of individuals who, in a desperate and even suicidal attempt to prevent war in Iraq, turned themselves into a human shield. They have now been punished along with, it must be said, the Iraqi population.

Opposition to war was not about Saddam Hussein. It is about the Iraqi population—men, women and children. No matter how sophisticated and smart the technology, weapons of war have a capacity to kill indiscriminately.

Time Europe ran a survey asking which country is the greatest threat to world peace. Of the more than 300,000 participants, 84 per cent picked the U.S., 8.63 per cent Iraq, 7.5 per cent North Korea.[3]

The Arabs should have exploited this and also the mounting criticism on Bush's handling of the U.S. economy and Iraq, and on the Security Council's ruptures over Iraq. Why can't the Arabs also listen to France, Germany, China and Russia and get them to side the Arabs?

The Arabs were defeated in the PR battle, too, despite being presented with opportunities. We saw how the Americans milked the 'ordeal' of Jessica Lynch. Sadly, the gripping tale of Ali Ismail Abbas, the 12-year-old boy who lost both arms and parents in a bombing on March 30, 2003, did not produce a big impact to capture the world's sympathy on the

---

3 *The Washington Post*, Jan. 28, 2003

Iraqis' suffering. The Arabs should have capitalised on it. Unfortunately, the Arabs did not look into Ali's welfare seriously and it took a foreigner, the Maharani of Jaipur, to sponsor his rehabilitation, thus amplifying the Arabs' indifference.

There was also this opinion that the Arab world should take advantage of the *Al-Jazeera* to broadcast to the Arab world to win support of Arab streets with the hope of changing the minds of their governments.

Saddam lamented that his neighbours "are more concerned about how an attack on Iraq would affect them domestically than with Iraq's welfare." *Time* magazine reported that Saudi Arabia was putting together the coup-package because "Riyadh fears that war in Iraq could lead to chaos, civil war among ethnic factions and military incursions by neighbours—Turkey and Iran." Curiously, no fears were expressed of long-term American, British or Israeli presence on Arab soil as a consequence of the invasion of Iraq.

Despite all the Arab League's common stances, they were not defending Iraq and its people nor the freedom and sovereignty of the Arab nations. It was disappointing that the Arab Governments behave as if they do not know there was a massive military build-up that eventually saw some 300,000 foreign troops on Arab land. Across the world, the opposition against the Iraqi war was greater than the Vietnam War protests. Yet the Arab leaders bowed to American pressure.

The late Palestinian-born scholar, Edward W. Said, writing in the Egyptian *Al-Ahram Weekly*: "How can a region of almost 300 million Arabs wait passively for the blows to fall, without attempting a collective roar of resistance, and a loud proclamation of an alternative view? Has the Arab will been completely dissolved?"

Many in the world were puzzled by this Arab inaction, mute voice and lack of desire to defend a fellow Arab country. To surrender without even a fight is the greatest shame to any race. Indeed was the Arab will being completely dissolved—or is it that Arabs are choosing to look the other way? I cannot provide an answer. It was not the Arabs who are trying to look the other way; it was their governments.

They seem to be perpetually manipulated by the powers-that-be of the world. It is amazing that a region that controls a third of the world oil output and reportedly invested hundreds of billion of dollars in the West, remain faithfully subservient to the U.S. and its allies. Unfortunately, in spite of the billions of oil revenue, the majority of the Arabs are poor.

Their Rulers allow themselves to be browbeaten, partly because of the desire of many to cling on to power by restricting democracy. UNDP's *Arab Human Development Report* 2002 listed three key deficits hampering growth in the region—made up of 22 countries in the Middle East and North Africa with a population of 280 million. These are freedom deficit, women's empowerment deficit and human capabilities/knowledge deficit relative to income.

These regimes survive in part due to the support of the West who is quite prepared to compromise its status as the paragon of democracy in return for the leverage it enjoys, to be used to twist Arab arms. The Iraqi situation is an example why the West had accommodated the Arab regimes.

A former British top diplomat told BBC's *HARDtalk*, that "Arab brothers are scared of the U.S., they fear they will be next". This was confirmed by King Abdullah of Jordan in a BBC interview after the war.

Henry Kissinger used to joke about how very dangerous it is to be America's enemy, but how inevitably fatal it is to be America's friend. Even if an Arab regime obliged the U.S. to protect itself, how could they ignore the threat of what increasingly appears to be but a thinly-veiled crusade against Islam?

Bush is a devout Christian. He took counsel from evangelist Tony Evans who recalls "one of the impetuses for his considering running for president was biblical teaching. He feels that God is talking to him. Bush introduced Bible study and prayers between Cabinet meetings."[4]

Ed Vulliamy wrote: "Now on the brink of war, George Bush has turned the 'vision thing' into an international crusade. On the world stage, his faith has done two things: First, it has welded a curious alliance between gritty, hard-headed Christians and the East Coast, moneyed, invariably intellectual, Zionist movement, making Ariel Sharon's Israel by far Bush's closest ally. Second, it has become a quest for unchallenged power."

Washington is not devoid of extremists, in the form of zealot backers of the Christian Right who will not be satisfied until they can change the faces of Mecca and Medina. By 'liberating' Iraq and bringing it to its side, the West anticipates the rest will meekly toe the line, unable to stand up to the combined forces of U.S./Israel plus, a new pro-West Iraq. It will be the old "domino theory" in reverse.

Against this background, commentators had high hopes for the Arab Summit in Manama in March 2003 where Saudi's "Charter to Reform the Arab Position" was supposed

---

4 *The Observer*, Jan. 25, 2003

to be discussed. The charter rejected "external aggression against any Arab State, guarantee safeguarding Arab legal interests, achieve just Arab demands, and work earnestly toward full implementation of a greater Arab free trade zone by the end of 2005."[5] But Arabs went to Manama to quarrel bitterly. This was showcased.

5 *Saudi Gazette*, Jan. 14, 2003

Chapter 4

DESPAIRING ARABS

> "There is a moral point to be made here. This war was about Iraq possessing illegal weapons of mass destruction—yet we are using weapons of mass destruction ourselves .... Such double standards are repellant."
>
> *Prof. Dough Rokke,*
> former Director of Pentagon's
> Depleted Uranium Project

BOOKS dissecting the Arab mind conveniently find them to be "depressed conspiracy theories". This stereotyping, I dare say, has tormented many an Arab soul. How could they not see conspiracies when ...?

- The French had throughout history been protective of the Christian Maronites in Beirut. During the French Mandate over Lebanon, a National Pact was introduced in 1943 detailing power-sharing among the ethnic groups. It favoured the Christians;
- The Arabs got a raw deal when the Arab world was carved out upon the breakup of the Ottoman Empire at the end of World War I in 1918-19.

Several new States were created—Syria, Lebanon, Jordan, Iraq—when, as Michael Field argued in his book *Inside the Arab World*: "... there was no neat cultural and historical logic to each of them that they could be easily accepted";[1]

- The Arabs were given instant States and Kings as in the case of Feisal, son of Sheriff Hussein of Mecca, and a confidante of Lawrence of Arabia during the Arab Revolt;
- The Zionists secured the 1917 Balfour Declaration from the British Government that promised British support for the creation of a Jewish State partly because the British Government reportedly thought the Jews controlled the Young Turks Movement, the German Government and the Russian Revolution;
- One minute after the British ended its Mandate on Palestine at 6p.m., Washington time on May 14, 1948, the State of Israel was established. Ten minutes later it was recognised by the U.S.;
- By the time of the British withdrawal, some 400,000 Arabs had fled their homeland. Among the tricks used by the Jews—secret radio stations broadcasting reports of spreading epidemics and alleged treachery of Arab leaders and their collaboration with the Zionists.

The fragility of the Arab States showed up rapidly. Iraq became what it was probably meant to be—a messy State, one that "required" the endless intervention by the British and then, the U.S.. Lebanon prospered for a few decades be-

---

1 Michael Field, *Inside the Arab World*, Harvard University Press, Cambridge, Mass., 1995

fore falling apart. I hope the lasting peace Lebanon now enjoys will set this small country on the road to success and prosperity once again.

After World War II, a new generation of military figures and politicians surfaced and they started overthrowing monarchies and regimes. This started in Syria in 1949, followed by Egypt in 1952, Iraq and Sudan in 1958, Yemen in 1962 and Libya in 1969. In due time, the new leaders started behaving as tyrannical rulers.

Little wonder that modern analyses of the Arabs talk about their political and economic failures. More changes can be expected. The Arabs despise their leaders. The Arab World is a youthful population; 38 per cent of them are under 14 years old.[2] Unless they see hope and opportunities they will be open to incitements and provocations. The widely discussed UNDP's *Arab Report* produced unnerving findings. Half of young Arabs polled want to emigrate! Is this about hatred for their Governments or an abiding love for everything Western?

The GDP of all Arab countries combined—$531.2 billion—is less than that of Spain at $595.5 billion. By 1998, the real purchasing power parity (PPP) income of the average Arab citizen had fallen to 13.9 per cent, or one-seventh of that of the average OECD citizen. Unemployment runs into double digits in most Arab countries. If unemployment is to be reduced to a manageable level by the year 2010, a minimum of 5 million jobs will have to be created every year.[3]

---

2 "Democracy: It Could Happen Here", Commentary by Stan Crock, *Business Week*, Dec. 23, 2002

3 The full report is available on the UNDP website.

Who do they turn to for help? Unless given access to oil, or air bases or a significant say in the management of their economies, the West will only pay lip service. Britain's Tony Blair was glad to host Syria's Bashar as-Assad after Syria stunningly voted with the rest for Security Council Resolution 1441 on Iraq. Writing in the *Financial Times* on the day of Bashar's visit in December 2002, Tony Blair observed:

> "The main author of Syria's information technology is a British consultant. We are giving advice on economic reform. The British Council is supporting Syria's universities. Scholarships are being provided for Syrian students to take postgraduate courses here (U.K.) so they have the expertise needed to help in the liberalising of their country".[4]

Blaming the West for all its failings will continue to be convenient. It will not mask the fact that the Arab/Muslim World has no cohesive strategies. Dr. Tariq Ramadan, the grandson of Hasan al Bana, recently asked:

> "Have we a strategy? We don't. We are totally divided because we have dictators. The reality of the Islamic world is dictatorships and there is no self-criticism. Even the people who are subject to this repression don't dare to speak."

The Arab/Muslim World has been unable to agree on many things—how to handle Osama bin Laden, the Gold

---

4 Tony Blair, "Engaging with Syria to undermine Iraq", *Financial Times*, Dec. 16, 2002

dinar, and oil as weapons. Indeed, more reasons for the U.S. to blackmail them or ride roughshod over them.

The inclination to disagree is virtually inherent; history is littered with examples. Efforts to rally the Muslims are not new. One of the earliest calls for *jihad* came in 1914, made by the Sultan of Turkey[5] against Britain, France and Russia. He described them as "merciless enemies of Islam". Some in the Arab-Muslim World opposed this, suspecting a German hand in the *jihad* rhetoric.[6] Tony Blair's article on Syria was appropriately entitled "Engaging with Syria to undermine Iraq", continuing the Western tradition of splitting Muslims.

Still the Arab-Muslim World hardly needs outside help to spite each other. The Palestinian Liberation Organisation (PLO) has had to seek new bases every now and then, having been evicted from Jordan following civil wars in 1970 and 1971; and from Beirut in 1983. There was a time when the PLO had its headquarters in Tunisia, a long way from Palestine.

Deceit and distrust grip relations in the Middle East. Nowhere else are neighbours so deeply distrustful of each other, for good reasons too. President Hosni Mubarak of Egypt survived an assassination attempt in 1995, which he blamed on neighbour, Sudan. Iraq and Iran slaughtered each other for eight long years. Bahrain perpetually fears Iran. Iraq invaded Kuwait. But Kuwait and the other Gulf nations also feared Iran. They got together in 1981, a year into the Iran-Iraq war, to form the Gulf Cooperation Council (GCC). GCC backed

---

5 Turkey and Iran are non-Arabs.

6 Lawrence James, *The Rise and Fall of the British Empire*, Abacus, London, 1994

Iraq, which turned around and mauled Kuwait. Just whom do you trust?

For years in the 1990s, the Arab leaders could not convene any full-scale meeting. Conflict is permanent in the region. Despite the U.K.'s and U.S.'s strong presence in the region, it has not dissipated. Thus the superpowers have an excuse to get more involved in putting the Arab world "right". It is the old "white man's burden" all over again, they sighed. U.S. Defense Secretary Donald Rumsfeld told Larry King in a December 2002 interview on CNN: "You can sense unrest in Iran." Incidentally, the role of one Michael Ledeen has been conspicuous with regards to Iran. He is American Enterprise Institute's Freedom Chair holder and one of the four advisers in regular contact with White House strategist Karl Rove. Ledeen and Sohrab Sobhani, an Iranian American, have recently established *The Coalition for Democracy in Iran* to promote regime change. The likes of Michael Ledeen had been rolled out to prove a supposedly clandestine al-Qaeda-Iran link. The self-assuredness of the neo-conservatives is frightening. Ledeen argued that the Iraq War was a regional one that must not stop at Iraq. It should be extended to cover Iran, Syria and Saudi Arabia. The war advocates are relentless in their pursuits, dodging controversies over the "missing" WMD to press ahead with regime changes in Syria and Iran. Danielle Pletka, like Ledeen from American Enterprise Institute,[7] was bellicose on television when told that the moral purpose of the war had been compromised without the WMD to show. "We found the chemical protection

---

7 The American Enterprise Institute is a recurring name throughout the war on terror. When Dick Cheney chose to break a long silence and put up a spirited display in justifying the invasion, he spoke at the American Press Institute on July 24, 2003.

gear," she said. The neo-conservatives have been winning all the arguments since.

They compelled the West to indulge in a fair bit of muck-raking and nitpicking to keep up the pressures on the Arab regimes. Cheques issued in the name of Princess Haifa al-Faisal, the wife of the Saudi Arabian Ambassador in Washington, dominated headlines for weeks. It prompted *The Wall Street Journal* to write a stinging editorial:

> "The September 11 attacks exposed the Saudi double game for all to see. And the entire American political system, including Congress, the media and especially the public, is now demanding that Riyadh do more than it has so far to track and intercept Saudi money going to Islamic groups that fund terror. Prince Bandar's problems isn't his wife's donations; it is Riyadh who need to decide whose side they are on".

Newsweek said this new "with us or against us" doctrine were causing anxieties among traditional allies of the U.S.. The Americans it seems have big plans for the Arabs. "There is a great potential for Saudi Arabia to look a lot more like the U.S. in 20 years," *Newsweek*, quoting a senior American official in Riyadh.

Iraq, the wrong target?

Muslims are troubled by the tone of the debate in Washington that increasingly suggests that Saudi and not Iraq should have been the target. Critics of the White House now say the war on terror had been derailed as a result of the invasion of Iraq.

Saudi has been also been blamed for Nine-eleven and funding of so-called terrorist organisations. Fifteen of the 19 suspected hijackers involved in Nine-eleven attacks were Saudis. Some believe it was deliberate on the part of Osama bin Laden. He had wanted to create a wedge between Saudi and the U.S.. A congressional report had 28 pages withheld by White House ostensibly over references to links between the hijackers and the Saudi ruling elite. Is this kind of intelligence less flawed and not as dodgy as the others?

Earlier in 2002, the Americans were stung by remarks and mutterings emanating from Riyadh about the need for Washington and Riyadh to go their separate ways. Pentagon's Defense Policy Board has been uncompromising in its assessments of Saudi.

I believe that following the mounting pressure, the White House will be tempted to pursue regime change in Riyadh too, albeit through a subtler approach. Perhaps that has always been the strategy; it is always safer to secure the alternative oil first, that is Iraq oil.

We are thus staring at a rearranged political structure in the Arab World. I have always wondered why despite the expanding middle class in the region, the Arab World seems cowed. The U.K.-U.S. axis had been around for decades, why didn't they sort out the mess earlier? Are they, in part, the cause of the mess?

The Middle East countries (for that matter their Central Asian neighbours too) have been too casual, trusting, reckless or simply too warlike in the foreign-diplomacy tone.

Contrast Saddam Hussein's fire-breathing pronouncements with the ease with which Turkey and the then Ruler of Libya had signed agreements to let the Americans use their airbases in 1954.[8] The Americans lured the House of Saud with a $25 million loan and a payment of $10 million for the lease of an airfield in Dharan. (By 1960, the U.S. had distributed $2,702 million to the Middle Eastern States.)[9]

The presence of U.S. bases had further weakened Arab unity. Syria under Hafez Assad was hostile to King Hussein's Jordan because the latter accommodated U.S. warplanes.

The lessons have not obviously been learned. The new Central Asian countries have been quick to accommodate U.S. bases. A Chicago-based biweekly magazine reported:

> "The State Department and Pentagon have quietly cobbled together a bold strategy for American military expansion into Central Asia, building military facilities in Kyrgystan, Uzbekistan and Tajikistan. And staking claim to a land of deserts, vast steppe and towering mountain ranges along the ancient Silk Road, where no Western country has ever stationed troops before."[10] In one neat move, the U.S. achieved its objective of turning the newly-independent Muslim nations of Central Asia into client-states as well as extend its military encirclement of the future threat, China."

---

8 Muammar Gaddafi's Revolutionary Command Council asked the U.S. to remove its forces from Libya's *Wheelus Field* Air Base when it ousted King Idris in 1969. Turkey's *Incirlik* Air Base was once strategic to the U.S. as Turkey shares 360 miles of common border with the former Soviet Union.

9 Lawrence James, *The Rise and Fall of the British Empire*, Abacus, London, 1994

10 J. Eric Duskin, "Permanent Installation", *The Times*, March 29, 2002

Middle East diplomacy is replete with missed opportunities. After World War II, the emerging world superpower, the U.S., eyed both the airfields and oil fields in the Middle East. The French, then Israel's closest ally, and Britain were on the retreat after being bled by the war. The U.S. was promoting itself as a benign power. Arab governments, had they been united, cohesive and far-sighted, could have secured favourable deals and structured better relationship with the U.S., instead of giving them air bases, which will eventually be used to threaten, police and attack them.

In fact, in the 1956 Suez Crisis, President Dwight Eisenhower had intervened to foil a scheme hatched by Britain, France and Israel to attack Egypt.

The episode and the rise of Gamal Nasser who took power with fellow Free Officers in 1952 at age 34, had stirred Arab Nationalism right across the Middle East.[11] Two weeks after Nasser forced the 80,000 British troops along the Canal to go home,[12] the Algerians launched an eight-year revolt to drive out the French. Britain was holding on to Iraq. Gamal Nasser nationalised the Suez Canal after the World Bank, America and Britain reneged on a promise of a $70 million loan for the Aswan High Dam.

---

11 Gamal Nasser is still idolised in the Arab World, 33 years after his death. Recent Arab Street protestors were chanting his name.

12 The troops were stationed in Suez to protect India. By the time Gamal Nasser came into power, India had gained Independence. The Canal was the creation of one of the earliest multinational companies —The Universal Company of the Maritime Suez Canal. Established in 1858, its directors were French, Belgian, American, Russian and Venetian. *The Economist* of June 14, 2003 reviewed a new book on the canal, *Parting the Desert: The Creation of the Suez Canal* by Zachary Karabell, Knopf.

Donald Neff writing in the July 1996 issue of *Washington Report on Middle East Affairs*, said of the Suez Crisis:

> "The plan was to 'pretend'* Israel had been hit by an Egyptian raid, and in retaliation its army would race across the Sinai Peninsula, and occupy the East Bank of the Suez Canal. In response, Britain and France would *'pretend' to stop a new Egyptian-Israeli war. All the while, of course, their warships and troops would actually be attacking Egypt." (*This 'pretend' game is still carried out by the superpowers, regardless of the innocent lives that the games have cost.)
>
> "Although facing presidential elections in November, Eisenhower publicly and privately opposed the three countries. Using every power short of military force at his command, Eisenhower compelled them to stop their naval bombardment and invasion of Egypt and withdraw without gaining any profit from their 'pretend' games. Not only did Nasser not fall, but his prestige soared in the Arab world as the leader who faced down the West and Israel."

The British Prime Minister Anthony Eden, until then the "unchallenged King of British politics" fell.[13] Britain lost Iraq to the nationalists in 1958. Algeria gained independence four years later.

It was the differences and disunity among the Arabs that continued to weaken their resolve in fighting Israel.

---

13 In an interview with *Al-Ahram Weekly* (Jan. 16-23 2003) British politician George Galloway said the Iraqi war could be Tony Blair's Suez. The right-wing newspaper, *The Daily Telegraph* subsequently accused Galloway of accepting payments from Saddam Hussein's regime. He bitterly contested the allegation.

The Jews were not exactly everyone's blue-eyed boy when they set up home in the Middle East. Many in the West were deeply contemptuous of the Jews who were often mentioned in the same breath as the Communists.

By 1939, there were 800,000 Arabs in Palestine, and under 200,000 Jews. The Jews were driven and united. The demography was quickly reversed. Another round of the Arab Revolt erupted. At the time of the 1948 partition, the Arabs appeared united. They went to war but were foiled by obsolete weapons. This was a reason that Nasser and friends took power. The disdain for Israel was a rallying cry.

The momentum collapsed in 1967 when Israel launched a pre-emptive strike. Egypt, Syria and Jordan were forced to go to war when their armies were not ready. The Egyptians had large numbers of forces in Yemen backing the anti-Saudi, anti-Royalist forces.[14] Israeli's French-equipped Air Force, destroyed 304 Egyptian aircrafts, 53 out of the 112 Syrian planes and all of Jordan's 28-aircraft air force. Jordan lost the West Bank and Arab East Jerusalem; Egypt, the Sinai Peninsula and Syria, the Golan Heights.[15]

---

14 Egypt, Syria and Iraq supported socialism. Saudi, Jordan and Morocco supported the West. Algeria was aloof.

15 Gamal Nasser offered to resign, but *The Daily Telegraph* report of the event said the crowd wanted him to stay. The British newspaper said Nasser insisted that Israel was assisted by the U.K. and U.S. Egypt's *Al-Ahram Weekly*, chronicling the Revolution later, said Nasser's close friend, and Commander-in-chief of the Armed Forces Field Marshall Abdel Hakim Amer was arrested and reportedly had committed suicide while in custody. Amer's children had bitterly contested the suicide-claim, saying their father had been poisoned. Nasser lumbered on but died of a heart attack in Sept. 1970, aged 52, at the end of a 1970 summit called to stop the fighting in Jordan between the Palestinians and King Hussein's forces.

By 1973 Anwar Sadat had gone to war with Israel, his limited success sufficient to boost Arab confidence. But in 1979, Anwar Sadat made peace with the Jewish State, the first Arab country to do so. It was a blow to the Arab League leading to Sadat's assassination two years later. For that gesture, America gave Egypt a yearly grant of $2 billion,[16] and Egypt's membership in the Arab League was suspended. The league's headquarters was moved from Cairo to Tunis.

The Arab humiliation, despair, anger and shame produced militants all over the Arab World. They were disillusioned and fed up with what they saw happening around them. They were completely demoralised.

Israel was on the ascendant. It exploited all the Arab differences and disunity. Importantly, the 1967 war permanently sealed the American perception of the Arab-Israeli conflict, or as Noam Chomsky put it, U.S./Israel-Palestine conflict. The U.S.-Israel relations improved dramatically after 1967.

Clear Thinking

The Arabs will continue to be outwitted by Israel unless they are united. The 1973 oil embargo worked because they were united. In fact, another British PM, Edward Heath, fell on his

---

16 To this day, the West is still trying to get the Arab world to recognise Israel. They are reportedly urging Crown Prince Abdullah of Saudi to "renew, before the elections (Jan. 28, 2003 elections in Israel), his sweeping offer of full Arab recognition of Israel in exchange for full withdrawal from all territories occupied in the 1967 war—which are heart of the struggle, wrote William Pfaff in the *International Herald Tribune*, "A U.S. road map to failure", Dec. 16, 2002

sword after the 1973 oil embargo.[17] In 1974, Britain concurrently faced a nationwide coal miners' strike. It lasted four weeks. The Government brought back the three-day working week first introduced in 1972.[18] Heath called a general election and was defeated. The Arabs had indeed tasted success.

Sadly, instead of building on the successes, they were soon fighting each other again. Senseless arms purchases ensued. Throughout the 1980s, the Gulf countries spent 15 per cent of their GDP on arms, and billions more on financing Iraq's war against Iran, handing back their oil surpluses in exchange for weaponry that is effective only when used against fellow Arabs. The Gulf Cooperation Council was unable to prevent the Iraqi invasion of Kuwait in 1990 that strengthened the U.S. hand in the Middle East.

Accommodating the U.S. bases had been a grave strategic error. It reduced the political leverage of the Arab-Muslim World. Minus its Middle East air bases, the U.S. would have been compelled to seek political solutions to the Iraqi crisis.

Neither has the Palestinian leadership been brilliant strategists. *Intifada* started well. Stones versus modern weaponry! The oppressed against the mighty oppressor! It ener-

---

17 It was led by Saudi Arabia. It came days after first Egyptian forces had attacked Israel from across the Suez Canal, and later the Syrians crossing the Golan Heights. OPEC had imposed an oil embargo on the U.S. and increased prices by 70 per cent to U.S.'s western European allies. Overnight, the price of a barrel to these nations rose from $3 to $5.11. In November 1973, President Richard Nixon extended the Daylight Savings Time and imposed a total ban on the sale of gasoline on Sundays.

18 From the website of the National Library of Wales

gised the Palestinian resistance, and gained a sympathetic world audience. But the strategy soon floundered.

Public opinion

The Israelis are master propagandists. Its media is filled with numbers, as they put a net value to the troubles wrought by *Intifada* on Israel. Published were numbers like the current Al Aqsa *Intifada* that started on September 29, 2000 unleashing 145 suicide bombers on Israel. *Intifada* wiped out 2.7 per cent of the GDP in 2001.

Don't the Palestinians have better strategies? You don't get anywhere killing innocent victims. The Jews will not suddenly flee Israel.

The Palestinian biggest hope is to have an Israeli Government that will talk peace. Yet in every election they don't allow Israelis to vote in the lesser of the two evils. By resorting to violence that begets violence, the Palestinians help install hard line Governments in Israel that will kill more Palestinians. U.S. will continue to back Israel. Modern-day Eisenhowers will be defeated in the American elections.

While strategically, they keep squandering the opportunities, the Palestinian cause is absolutely legitimate. There is no lack of international support for the cause.

In a memo to *New York Times* columnist Thomas L. Friedman, Nelson Mandela said: "The Palestinian-Israeli conflict is not just an issue of military occupation and Israel is not a country that was established 'normally' and happened to occupy another country in 1967. Palestinians are not struggling for a 'state' but for freedom, liberation and equality, just like we were struggling for freedom in South Africa".

"Apartheid is a crime against humanity. Israel has deprived millions of Palestinians of their liberty and property and has perpetuated a system of gross racial discrimination and inequality. It has systematically incarcerated and tortured thousands of Palestinians, contrary to the rules of international law. It has in particular waged a war against a civilian population, in particular children".

I believe the Palestinian cause is dependent on Arabs' ability to exercise its leverage.

A Return of the Oil Weapon?

Oil remains a potent weapon. When Iraq advocated this in 2002 to punish Israeli's belligerence and U.S.'s inertia in the Israeli-Palestinian conflict, many western media reports asked: "Will oil be a weapon in the Middle East conflict?" They don't quite like the spectre. Although another oil embargo would punish producers' economies that rely on oil revenues, the jitters were palpable.

The strategy of holding the world hostage to one's plight, no matter how just and desperate, is not one that wins friends and influences people. But I also happen to believe in countries and groupings working on their collective leverage. When one force cancels the other, one cannot dominate the other. Stability will be preserved, and situations that will cause economic devastations such as war, will be avoided. Oil is therefore a means of conflict resolution.

Oil may not be as effective an instrument of peace as it was in 1973. Then, OPEC controlled half of the world's market share. This may have dipped to one-third but that does not mean an oil strategy will not bite. The cover of *Fortune* magazine (December 2, 2002) declared: "After Saddam—If all goes well, oil will flow and the global economy will prosper. If not, watch out."

The U.S. Department of Energy announced at the beginning of January 2003 that by Year 2025, U.S. oil imports would account for perhaps 70 per cent of total U.S. domestic demand. (It was 55 per cent in 2001.) As Michael Renner of the Worldwatch Institute put it bleakly, "U.S. oil deposits are increasingly depleted, and many other non-OPEC fields are beginning to run dry. The bulk of future supplies will have to come from the Gulf region." Some 70 per cent of the world's proven oil reserves are in the Middle East. The number of years that reserves of oil will last at current production rates—compiled by Jeremy Rifkin in *Hydrogen Economy*, in the U.S., where more than 60 per cent of the recoverable oil has already been produced, the ratio is just 10 years, as it is in Norway. In Canada, it is 8:1. In Iran, it is 53:1, in Saudi Arabia 55:1, in the United Arab Emirates 75:1. In Kuwait, it's 116:1. But in Iraq, it's 526:1. And this forthcoming war isn't about oil?[19]

While oil was the catalyst for waging war, there were other motives. Consider this: "If you look at a map, Iraq is the most strategic country between the Levant and the Persian Gulf. It shares borders with Jordan, Syria, Turkey, Iran, Kuwait and, most of all, Saudi Arabia. If the U.S. were to occupy Iraq, it would be there by right of conquest. Unlike any other country in the region, the U.S. would not have to negotiate with an occupied Iraq. It would have ample room for deploying air power in the heart of the region. More important, it would be able to deploy a substantial ground force ca-

---

19 Robert Fisk, "This looming war isn't about chemical warheads or human rights, it's about oil", *Independent*, Jan. 18, 2003

pable of bringing pressure to bear within a 360-degree radius. Within a matter of months, the U.S. would become the most powerful military force native to the region."[20]

Many have written and given their views, and here are some thoughts as to how the Arabs and Muslims can raise their world standing and self-esteem:

- Arabs must think as Arabs first, given the common culture, language and religion. In the eyes of the West, Gamal Nasser became a potent threat after he wrote the book *Revolt on the Nile*. Every embassy was reported to have read the book. Nasser wanted to unite the Arabs, transform Arab World to be a force to be reckoned;
- Saudi should emerge as a medium-size regional economic and military power. The Arabs should also have a common Army, develop a strong defence industry, a common market and a common currency. Gamal Nasser tried but his undoing was his devotion to command economy. Gamal was pro-Russia and was seen as anti-American. Under Richard Nixon, Israel and Iran became America's dual pillars of regional stability, for a time acting as watchdogs over Gamal Nasser and his Arab nationalism. Moreover, Israel and Iran were seen as the ultimate defence against Soviet forays into the region;
- They should not be fighting their own Arab brothers, like in Algeria;

---

20 The War after Iraq: Strategic Forecasting (Stratfor)

- Muslim scientists should be encouraged to make groundbreaking discoveries. Malaysia has a committee whose aim is to produce world-class scientists who will go on and win such awards as the Nobel Prize. There is certainly no lack of talents in the Arab-Muslim world. Egyptian-born Prof. Ahmed Zewail won the Nobel Prize for Chemistry, the second Muslim to win the coveted prize;
- The Arabs must be very disciplined and acquire knowledge;
- Learn to earn self-respect and develop steely resolve. Hosni Mubarak was reported as saying "Nobody can stop America from attacking Iraq." Similar sentiments were expressed by King Abdullah of Jordan. This is a defeatist attitude. They seem to have fallen into Sharon's trap. Sharon's goal "was to create in the Arabs a psychology of defeat, to beat them every time and to beat them so decisively that they would develop the conviction that they would never win." The Americans believe they too can achieve this. Once they have defeated Iraq, the whole Arab world would just surrender;
- Muslims organisations should support the *ummah* in the manner the Jews support each other;
- Bring back all investments overseas. If they were to invest at home, there will be foreign capital inflows. With investments, comes employment. Some huge figures had been mentioned as to the extent of Arab money invested in the West. One estimate had it that Arabs have something like $650 billion in Europe and $975 billion in the U.S. Muhammad Omar Al-Amoudi writing in the *Arab News*, said if

> this was true the *zakat* would come to almost $60 billion. Other estimates vary. Some say the total Arab investments abroad is $650 billion. Whatever it is, *zakat* is Muslim strength. And what are the Arabs doing enriching the Westerners who are managing their funds abroad? *The Economist* observed shrewdly: "... the image of Arabs wallowing in wanton luxury abroad persists."

Enlightened Arab commentators now worry about the consequences of the "enrichment and aggrandisement" of the Arab leadership. A long line of foreign exploiters had taken advantage from this inherent weakness; Britain, France, Russia to America. They will pounce again. The Arabs will have to decide their fate. Their future is in their own hands. Either they better themselves or they can leave it to others to do it for them. The choice is theirs.

Chapter 5

BAGHDAD FELL (AGAIN)

> "The people of England have been led in Mesopotamia into a trap from which it will be hard to escape with dignity and honour. They have been tricked into by a steady withholding of information. The Baghdad communiqués are belated, insincere, incomplete. Things have been far worse than we have been told, our administration more bloody and inefficient than the public knows. It is a disgrace to our imperial record, and may soon be too inflamed for any ordinary cure. We are today not far from a disaster .... How long will we permit millions of pounds, thousands of Imperial troops, and tens of thousands of Arabs to be sacrificed on behalf of colonial administrators?
>
> *Lieutenant Col. Thomas Edward Lawrence (a.k.a. Lawrence of Arabia)*, in an article in *The Sunday Times* of London dated August 22, 1920, regarding England's occupation of ancient lands in the Middle East

ARABS have been left rudderless and defeated. Worse, we have come across that line before in the stupefying history of the Arabs.

As the war advocates defend their assertions that Saddam Hussein kept dangerous amount of biological and chemical weapons, what did the Arab rulers do? They retreated to the sidelines. Is there a way out of the bind for the Arabs?

Normalcy has not been restored since Baghdad, once a cradle of civilisation, is once again under foreign rule although this one said they would devolve power to locals.

Baghdad had once been the largest and the most civilised city in the world. Multiple invasions precipitated its decline. Can Baghdad ever recover? I have absolute faith in the tenacity of the people of Baghdad.

History is on their side, at least on achievements of their ancestors. Water and security are scarce in post-Saddam Baghdad. Ancient Baghdad had free hospitals, public baths, a postal service, a water supply, a sewage system as well as banks.

The most recent invaders of Baghdad behave as if the city popped up yesterday without institutions and traditions; they are getting a lot of help from the looters and offenders who are giving Iraqis and Muslims a bad name. Iraq deserves more respect. Under Caliph Harun Al-Rashid, Baghdad lorded over an Islamic empire that included North Africa, Palestine, Syria, Iraq to beyond Persia, Afghanistan, and to Azerbaijan and to the South of the Caspian Sea.

Baghdad is the birthplace of Abraham, father of three religions. Baghdad had a College of Translators in 833AD established by Caliph Mamun. The intellectuals of the day had churned out a wealth of knowledge by translating works in Greek, Syria, Persian and Sanskrit into Arabic. Caliph Mamun also established a Great Hall of Science with its library and astronomical library in Baghdad.

The Muslims were centuries ahead of the West. By the time the crusaders first achieved sword contact with the Islamic world, a scientist had correctly calculated the distance from Earth to Moon. Another, Jabir bin Hayya, had suggested that if the atom could be split, it might release enough power to destroy a city the size of Baghdad. Arab medicine was also highly developed. To practise medicine one was required to have knowledge of surgery, anatomy and the circulation of blood. There were specialists on eye surgery, brain tumours, epilepsy, preventive medicines and perhaps most important of all hygiene. Arab doctors even used anesthetic. By the time the Coalition of the Willing had finished with Baghdad, Iraqi surgeons had to operate without anesthetic amid mounting civilian casualties.

The Arab Street[1] is not without a history of resistance. They had endured Western or rather Christian aggression before. Winston Churchill, who merged three Ottoman provinces to become Iraq, had in his lifetime extolled the virtues of Christian Civilisation.

In their latest military pursuit, the British had joined forces with a few Australians in backing the Americans led by a president who is a born-again Christian. Was the Iraq War a clash of civilisations? Even if it was one, the Arab leaders preferred capitulation to defending their sovereignty.

This was the question that haunted many Arabs in the past. Despite being a sophisticated society, they were slow to respond to the Christian aggression from the West. Two or three thousand belligerent European Christians were able to establish a seat of Government in Jerusalem, as a precursor to today's Israel. The crusaders had then come not to merely extract tribute and taxes but to impose their own civilisation and their own brand of Christianity as opposed to Orthodox Greek, Georgian, Armenian and Jacobite. In today's language, "taxes" is oil and "civilisation" is culture, religion, freedom and democracy.

The crusade was an invasion; it was a colonisation war by one civilisation against another.

---

1 I make a distinction between Arab Street and the Arab leaders.

It is the same now. The troubles in American-ruled Iraq must not wickedly serve as a consolation. It will not change the fate of the Arabs who will further their cause better by exposing and articulating the web of lies spun by the aggressors.

At the U.N., Bush and Blair had blamed Iraq for not complying with U.N. Resolutions as if only Iraq did not comply. When few people bought the argument, the reasons to declare war were rapidly shifted causing greater confusion. In the end, Blair invoked the moral issue. If moral is a reason to go to war, the world would have wars all the time. Who is the arbiter to decide on the moral issues? Tony Blair?

I have always found Blair's war-mongering streak incredulous. By backing George Bush ferociously, he alienated his own Labour Party and the media that would ordinarily not be hostile to him—among them *The Independent, The Guardian* and the BBC. George Bush's foreign policy carries distinct domestic agendas. Pandering to the Jewish voters by eliminating Israel's biggest enemy ahead of an election year, shall do Bush no harm.

Draw no comfort from Blair's political troubles. It changes nothing because Blair decides nothing. Worse, the fall of Blair may precipitate the return of a more right-wing Conservative Party that may actually start wars rather than faithfully backing one as Blair did.

The Iraq War was manufactured in Washington. If the real perpetrators were not held to account, they would be free to inflict more torment. They are the neo-conservatives of Washington. The neo-conservatives have invaded our collective consciousness. They appear to be the most motivated and influential tribes ever to operate in Washington.

They are vilified and loved in equal measure. *The New Yorker* had much fun satirising the neo-con's Iraq link, naming a fictitious character Salim al-Wolfowitz. They had always wanted America to depose Saddam Hussein to start a domino of Arab democracies that they think will dramatically improve Israel's security. They suspiciously shape American foreign policy, in upgrading the U.S. from a hyper-power to an imperial power, or as some conceitedly argued, "liberal imperialism".

That Osama is out there has helped the cause of the neo-conservatives to rearrange the world in Israel's favour. They could always accuse any country to be working with Osama and al-Qaeda, thus warranting regime change.

The neo-conservatives wanted this war, but others chose not to stand in the way, among them the Arab regimes. Prince Bandar bin Sultan insisted that if the Arabs had opposed the war, their opportunity to shape post-Saddam Iraq would be lost. Questions—What is Saudi's role in the reconstruction of Iraq? Have any of Arab leaders been invited to Washington or Bush's ranch since the U.S. president declared the war to be over in April 2003?

Yet with the exception of Syria, the Arabs facilitated the invasion. Kuwait let the invaders use the air bases of Ali Salem and Ahmed Al Jaber for its fighter bombers, Stealth bombers, tank busters and Apache and Blackhawk helicopters. The Americans were in Camp Doha too. Centcom and General Tommy Franks were based in Qatar, home of *Al-Jazeera*. Bahrain houses U.S.'s 5th Fleet. United Arab Emirates and Jordan cooperated while Egypt gave the invaders air passage and the Suez Canal. Iran opted to be neutral.

If the Arabs had governed well and genuinely enjoyed the support of their people, the regimes would not have been at the mercy of the U.S.. Their frailties further weaken the cause of the Arabs. By 2003, they had been powerless to even entertain an oil embargo to prevent the invasion and colonisation of Iraq. Iraq remains a colony of the U.S. (and Britain) until the 145,000 troops leave, and they are not in a hurry to. The presence of the troops is essential for the peace and stability of Israel. If democracy produces a Shia clergy rule, will the Americans accept the outcome graciously?

History, meanwhile, is pregnant with tales of conspirators ditched by occupiers doubting their loyalties and uprightness. I shall not be judgmental of Chalabi's intentions. But his Iraqi National Congress did provide considerable intelligence to the Americans to undermine Saddam's regime. Tales spun by the Iraqi exiles were swallowed by American intelligence. Colin Powell has latterly said he spent four days and nights burrowing through CIA documents before presenting new evidence to the U.N. Security Council on February 5 2003. Sleeplessness and doggedness are no proofs of truth—was it wishy-washy evidence marketed by the Iraqi exiles that Powell quoted?

This is 2003. For decades now, many countries, poor and rich believe colonisation will never surface its ugly head again. We have all been proved wrong. From the pages of history, the powerful will always remain greedy. Expansion was one way of keeping the various forces busy and at the same time enriching themselves.

The Chalabis of the world had been forewarned. In the early 20th century, the U.S. journalist John Reed warned: "Uncle Sam never gives something for nothing". He said in a speech: "Anyone who accepts Uncle Sam's promises at face value will find that they must be paid for in sweat and blood."

Nor is peace in Middle East that Blair had committed Bush into, any nearer. Not with the blustery of Ariel Sharon, not with Jewish settlers egging him to be more ruthless and not with the escalation of violence since President Bush tried to get Israel and Palestine make peace. In the final analysis, the Iraq War presented Muslims everywhere with a devastating defeat. Arabs had to contend with Christian aggression in the past. Now the Christian Right has ganged up with the powerful Jewish lobby.

War in the Middle East is history itself. Baghdad had been conquered by the Turks, the Mongols, the British (World War I and British again in World War II) until the coup by the Free Officers in 1958 to topple the monarchy, which was installed and propped up by the British.

Malaysia gained Independence in 1957. Over in the Middle East then, Arab nationalism and unity rose to a crescendo. Similarly, the crushing defeat at the hands of the Crusaders brought together voices demanding a concerted response by the entire Arab world. There was this problem, though. There was no such thing as a united Arab world in the 11th century. It is worse now, of course. North Africa had split away when the Fatimids (claimed descendants from the Prophet's daughter, Fatimah) came to power and the Seljuks had taken control of everything. They were no Arabs.

Baghdad remained the national centre of authority, the home of the Caliphs. But the Turk overlord took the title "Sultan". In the three years after the fall of Jerusalem, Baghdad changed hands eight times as sons of Malik Shah fought for supremacy. The city was as it is today in chaos. (The American death toll after the fall of Saddam is rising).

When Caliph Umar captured Jerusalem from the Christians in the 638, he had assured the Patriach Christian, lives and property would be respected. He then requested a tour of the Christian holy site. When invited to unroll his prayer mat in the Church of Holy Scripture, he refused out of respect for Christians. A treaty was signed which previously listed the legal rights of Christians: "This peace guaranteed the security for lives, property, churches and the crucifixes belonging to those who displayed and honoured them. There shall be no compulsion in matters of faith."

The crusaders took a different approach. Fulcher of Chartres wrote: "Our squires and footmen can split open the bellies of those they had just slain in order to extract from the intestines the gold chain they had gulped down their loathsome throats while alive." The crusaders took possessions of houses and palaces as the case now where contracts largely went to well-connected American companies.

Fulcher of Chartres went on: "The crusaders forced an entry into the Al-Aqsa mosque and despite the protection of Tanscred's banner (leader of crusaders) flying above the building, slew everyone there, men, women and children— among them large numbers of Imams and Muslim scholars, ... men who had left their homeland to live lives of pious seclusion in the holy place. The same synagogue in which Jews sought shelter was set on fire and everyone in it, were burnt alive. It was ritual slaughter. They ordered the corpses to be thrown outside the city because of the terrible stench, for almost the whole city was full of dead bodies."

Killing was always wrong in the eyes of the Church. You commit a sin by killing and had to do penance for it. But killing, the Pope declared during the crusading, need not be a sin at all. Fighting for Pope's causes was not only an obligation, it made you righteous and with that one idea, the crusaders were set in motion. Papal supremacy had always been at the heart of crusading as American supremacy and imperialism is at the heart of a new empire. Crusade was a war on behalf of Rome. Today it is waged on behalf of America. Blair and John Howard are followers. The Pope's supposed authority to unlock the gates of heaven turned their troops into a state of murderous trance. Today their fighting forces think they are unlocking gates of freedom, democracy and globalisation even if it means using threats, bribery and breaking international law.

Chapter 6

THE JEWISH STORY

"The Jewish people began their search for freedom more than 3,000 years ago. From the struggle of the Exodus, to the miracle of the Maccabees, to the horrors of the Holocaust, to the creation of the democratic State of Israel, Jews have faced and survived many challenges ... Many Jewish Americans serving in our Armed Forces are working to rid the world of terror and bring freedom and justice to the oppressed."

George W. Bush,
on Jewish Heritage Week, 2003

HOLLYWOOD provides some clues into the influence wielded by the Jews. It helps us understand why the Road to Jerusalem goes through Baghdad, to fathom how the presence of 145,000 American troops will actually bolster Israel, and as Joe Klein, author of *Primary Colours*, wrote in the *Time* magazine of February 10, 2003: "A stronger Israel is very much embedded in the rationale for war with Iraq."

Roman Polanski's *The Pianist* (2002), unsurprisingly much-acclaimed, is the latest Hollywood depiction of the "sufferings" of the Jews. A new movie on the Jewish sufferings is practically made every few years.

Strange this, the perpetual Arab-Israel conflict has continuously failed to excite the Hollywood studios when it "remains the prism through which the Arabs see the United

States."[1] The Arabs? Well, they are the rogues, scoundrels and wicked, blood-sucking thieves; indeed a scandalous stereotyping. The Israelis are more vicious and brutal but even the Arabs have not remembered to make a movie on the killings at the Shabila and Shatila camps of 1982.

David Lean's *Lawrence of Arabia* (1962) spotlighted the gallant English colonel, T.E. Lawrence, who amplified his role in the Arab Revolt of 1917 in a book called the *Seven Pillars of Wisdom*.

The Arab Revolt was, now that we have the benefit of history, needless as the big powers of the time had decided to carve out the Arab World for themselves a year earlier. The Ottoman Empire was crumbling when the Arab Revolt, fanned by the British, erupted. In the 1916 Skyes-Picot Agreement, Sir Mark Sykes of Britain and Georges Picot of France ensured perpetual Arab turmoil by an arrogant division of Arab land into areas where "France and Great Britain shall have priority of right of enterprise and local loans"[2] and where the two powers "shall alone supply advisers or foreign functionaries at the request of the Arab state or confederation of Arab States".

A year after the Skyes-Picot Agreement came the Balfour Declaration that was touted as a British commitment to a Jewish State in Palestine, unleashing a wave of Jewish influx into the Arab land.

The Jews managed to pull off the Balfour Declaration, which was a brief non-binding note from James Balfour, the Foreign Secretary to Lord Rothschild, who promptly circu-

---

1 Shibley Telhami, "Mideast Peace?: An Arab-Israeli Pact Must Come First", *New York Times*, April 12, 2003

2 The agreement is readily available on the Internet.

lated the note they decided to call a Declaration. While the Jews are brutally masters of sound bites and propaganda, the conventional wisdom at the time suggested that Britain had its own geopolitical interest in backing the creation of a Jewish State. Britain saw Israel as bulwark against Arab nationalism and to keep its route to India open and safe. Such stratagem did not prevent the disintegration of the British Empire.

World attention on the Jewish power then shifted to the U.S. where many of New York's voters are Jews. The Jewish lobby at Capitol Hill more often than not gets what they want—including the signatures of Congressmen and Senators protesting the newly unveiled Road Map. Such is the undying American love for Israel that the enemies of the Jewish State are likely to make U.S.'s list of Rogue States. There are Jews who are no trenchant supporters of Israel; the likes of eccentric MIT professor Noam Chomsky.

Pray tell, though, how does a nation of roughly 4 million Jews (reinforced by 500,000 Russian Jews after the collapse of Soviet Union) could survive in a sea of 280 million mostly hostile Arabs? About a people who revived an ancient language Hebrew, not spoken widely in 2,000 years, to be the national language of their brand new country. A factual error in the main American newspapers when reporting on Israel will get corrected instantly, before the second edition is printed. Someone would surely call the newspapers. The Jews have practically turned Washington and New York into their dominions.

They keep delaying peace initiatives. Observe the old trick of its Prime Ministers not willing to sit down to discuss peace if there are seven or so clear days of non-violence, only for Israel to wade into the Occupied Territories[3] to commit more atrocities.

Dithering and procrastination have worked for Israel; each time their American backers try to get them to sit down and talk peace with the Palestinians, they belch out endless excuses. In the meantime, they expand the Jewish Settlements in the West Bank and East Jerusalem, home to 2.2 million Palestinians. Ariel Sharon through various Cabinet posts in the past two decades had been the biggest promoter of the Jewish Settlements. There is a lingering suspicion of Israeli ultimate goal of driving the Palestinians away, euphemistically termed as "transfer".

The number of Jewish Settlements, now central in the Road Map, has risen dramatically over the past 36 years or so. Some 376,000 Israelis live there attracted by lavish Government incentives and fortified by maximum security. The presence of the Jewish Settlements had significantly eroded the quality of life of the Palestinians, and brought despair and humiliation to the Palestinians. This is deliberate to drive home the message that the Palestinians are a defeated people. Changes in the road system tailored to benefit the Jewish settlers, suffocate the Palestinians. The *National Geographic* of October 2002 said: "Palestinians contemplating the 25-mile journey from Ramallah to Jericho, for example, must be prepared to spend an entire day, sometimes days, negotiating the various Israeli roadblocks and checkpoints along the way." The recent construction of the 5-metre-wide

3 The West Bank, East Jerusalem and the Gaza Strip were occupied by Israel in 1967 after the Six-Day War. An *intifada* of Palestinians against Israeli occupation, which began in 1987, ended when the Israeli government and Yasser Arafat, signed the Declaration of Principles in Sept. 1993.

wall will eventually snake for 900km along the West Bank. It is a land grab that will further terrorise the Palestinians. *Islamonline* reports: "The separation wall, which incorporates a network of earthworks, trenches and patrol roads, also cuts a whole string of Palestinian communities into two. The wall has infuriated Palestinians as it leaves large swathes of the occupied territory on the Israeli side and is seen as a bid to preempt negotiations on the final borders of the Palestinian state promised by 2005 under a U.S.-backed peace roadmap."

Successive Israeli Governments would move mountains to protect the settlements or to put up more. The issue of Settlements crops up in all peace initiatives only to be frustrated by Jewish stonewalling. They would delay and foil.

For example, in 1995, Arafat-Shimon Peres talk was delayed over the control of Hebron; Israel was reluctant to pull off its troops safeguarding the 415 Jewish settlers in Central Hebron who are surrounded by 120,000 Palestinians. After the signing of the Wye agreement, more "hilltop" settlements popped up.

Now, the Road Map is in the hands of Ariel Sharon who told the Press in March 2002: "The Palestinians must be hit hard and it must be very painful. We must cause them losses, victims, so that they feel the heavy price."[4]

A wave of violence quickly threatened to derail the Road Map. The Israelis are killing Palestinians militants by firing missiles on cars! They had also used fighter jets, and routinely deployed armoured personnel carriers (APCs) and Apache helicopters.

---

4 See Amnesty International online

Observed *Amnesty International*: "The military operations we have investigated appear to be carried out not on military purposes but instead to harass, humiliate, intimidate and harm the Palestinian population. Either the Israel army is extremely ill-disciplined or has been ordered to carry out acts which violate the laws of war."

The Americans seem not to be unduly worried. In fact before they invaded Iraq, some 1,000 U.S. soldiers went to Israel for joint manoeuvres and others were sent to a mock Arab town in Negev to draw on Israel experience of using bulldozers to demolish and clear streets. Pentagon strategists repeatedly watched videos of Israel bloody military assault on Jenin and have focused on learning Israel tactics of blowing holes in houses to facilitate house-to-house troop movement.

The sufferings inflicted on Palestinians were lost on the military planners or strategists. Said the *Amnesty International* report: "In every refugee camp they occupied, Israeli soldiers left a trail of destruction. Tanks roam over parked cars, broke down walls and house fronts and knocked down lamp-posts and street signs. Sometimes they rolled for no apparent reason into the front of houses. Electricity, water and telephones were cut for as long as the Israeli army remained in occupation. Meanwhile, wall-piercing bullets and sometimes tank rounds were shot for no apparent reason into shop fronts or houses."

Herein lies the deep-rooted anger towards the Americans. The long-suffering Arabs see the U.S. as a conspirator.

The behaviour of a group of neo-conservative faction in Washington had further deepened the link between the backers of Israel and policymakers in the heart of Washington; these officials can't draw a line between U.S. strategic interests and that of Israel.

Protecting strategic interests of Israel has always been the chief aims of the Likudniks such as Richard Perle. In a 1996 report "Clean Break", Perle mapped out a plan to protect Israel's strategic interests by reshaping the Middle East, starting with a regime change in Iraq. Now that the Americans are present in the Middle East in such overwhelming fashion, Israel is deemed to be safer. Perle is one of those who believe the domino effect of a democratic Iraq in the Arab World would give Israel lasting peace. They believe a democratic Arab will make peace with Israel. They believe the Americans will see to it that no mid-size Arab power will emerge to rival Israeli hegemony.

The hardline Jewish Institute for National Security Affairs can count on the backing of Perle and Dick Cheney. Also an ally was Jay Garner, the interim chief re-constructor of Iraq before he was replaced by Paul Bremer, a Henry Kissinger's protege. Jay Garner, a friend of Rumsfeld, was a signatory to a Jewish Institute statement that said: "Israel has exercised remarkable restraint in the face of lethal violence orchestrated by the leadership of the Palestinian Authority."

The Jewish Institute executive director Thomas Neumann believed that the Bush Administration is the best administration for Israel since Harry Truman who first recognised an independent Israel. Bush openly supported Sharon's stance in making the removal of Yasser Arafat as a condition of diplomacy. Indeed Israel gets whatever it wants, especially American acquiescence to its procrastination and atrocities.

Chapter 7

PRIZE OF WAR

"Every gun that is made, every warship launched, every rocket fired, signifies in the final sense a theft from those who hunger and are not fed, those who are cold and not clothed."

President Dwight D. Eisenhower
April 16, 1953

PENTAGON had devised a strategy of inviting punters to make money by betting on whether or not terrorist attacks, missile attacks, assassinations or coups would take place. Such wager, in a strange way, will help the U.S. ward off future shocks. Pentagon was forced to scrap this *Policy Analysis Market* proposed by a Pentagon unit, called *Defense Advanced Research Projects Agency* (DARPA) following hoots of derision from Capitol Hill.

I bet punters would have been unable to decide if it is safe to gamble on a war erupting every 10 years or so—Korea, Vietnam, Gulf War and now Iraq given the level of self-belief and "sense of mission" in Washington these days.

Researchers, punters and analysts at the *Policy Analysis Market* would have undoubtedly looked at Saddam Hussein's role in the U.S. economy—especially all those calls for a repeat of oil embargo and his "impudence" of changing the sacrosanct U.S. dollar with the emerging Euro. That 80 per cent of foreign exchange transactions are dominated in dollars means the rest of the world will have to provide America with goods and services in exchange for U.S. dollar.

U.S. imports may exceed export but it does not hurt as the strength of U.S. dollar provides a subsidy for its purchases. Euro will threaten the currency's pre-eminence if countries start opting for Euro reserves or trade in Euro. Then it is Europe's turn to enjoy the subsidy secured through the strength of its currency. Is U.S. going to roll over and let its strategic interests wiped out?

Without exception, nations pursue their own interests; paradoxically, America is spending $75 billion to "liberate" the people of Iraq when there are 3 million unemployed Americans. Pentagon officials said the supposedly benign U.S. would pay for the two million or more Iraqi bureaucrats and soldiers in the reconstruction phase (*The Washington Post*, March 12, 2003). In the run-up to the war, the U.S. economy was bleeding from the mega-sized corporate scandals and was in a real danger of a double-dip recession.

Will America bear the entire cost of waging war in Iraq? On the contrary, it stands to gain from the war with the overall reconstruction costs to exceed $30 billion in the first three years as estimated by the U.N. For starters, the U.S. paid just $12 billion out of the $61 billion consumed by Gulf War I—the Gulf States had to fork out $36 billion, monies that could have earned the Arab States something like 10 KLIAs; after which the Arabs had to buy weapons that crippled their economies. The Arab regimes continued to back America despite the rise of anti-Americanism in the Arab Street.

Back in 1991, Colin Powell, the then-chairman of U.S. Joint Chiefs of Staff, favoured "overwhelming force" that required considerably more troops than what U.S. Defense Secretary Donald Rumsfeld, a former CEO, envisaged under his own leaner-troop doctrine. There have been calls for reinforcements, including by the likes of William Cohen former Defence Secretary. Already Pentagon estimates the cost of keeping 145,000 American troops in Iraq to be at $3.9 billion a month.

Bush has long been advised that the war should be financed by Iraqi oil money. A large sum of money has been accrued under the Oil-for-Food programme, held in trust by U.N. How will they spend it? Until the stoppage of the programme, Russian and French firms and banks had benefited from the scheme; which curiously needed intermediaries for the purchase of food for Iraq. That was a scheme to ensure the support of the two Security Council members.

Reports suggest that the economic beneficiaries from the miseries of Iraqis will be mostly American companies. Lots of contracts to rebuild roads, schools and hospitals are to be awarded. The plan as unveiled before the war was to repair 3,000 schools and provide supplies to 12,500 schools. Some 550 diesel generators were supposed to be installed within 60 days. Yet, the Bush Administration had set aside a pitiful $1.7 billion for the reconstruction of Iraq which according to U.S. Budget Director, Joshua B. Bolten would cost $7.3 billion this year.

The rebuilding contracts, unsurprisingly, were initially disbursed by the U.S. Agency for International Development. AFP, the French wire service, reported on March 28 2003, the Americans had awarded a $4.8 million job to rebuild Iraq's only deep-water port to Stevedoring Services of America. It was said to be one of the eight contracts for initial rebuilding valued at $900 million.

Severe criticisms of such decisions mean we have not heard of any since. Halliburton was however reported to be in the running for 21-month contract to reconstruct Iraq's infrastructure, including roads, bridges and hospitals. A denial was issued ostensibly to quell criticisms of cronyism. That may not prove too successful. Kellogg Brown & Root (KBR), its subsidiary, had secured the job of dealing with oil-well fires in Iraq without bidding.

That Halliburton has close links with the White House is common knowledge. Vice President and former Defence Secretary Dick Cheney was CEO of Halliburton for five years till the late 1990s, when KBR "provided all the food, water, laundry, mail and heavy equipment to the roughly 20,000 U.S. troops stationed in the Balkans .... The military has paid KBR $3 billion." (*Fortune*, March 17, 2003). Alongside his former mentor, Donald Rumsfeld, Cheney was a fierce advocate of the Iraqi invasion. The *Financial Times* profiled Cheney it its March 22/23 edition under the heading "*The figure in the White House shadows who urged the president to war in Iraq*". The article observed: "Just before becoming vice president, he [Cheney] was chief executive of Halliburton, the energy group, returning to Washington $36m richer."

Will America be richer in post-Iraq? That the Iraqi exercise underscores an economic pursuit has always been palpable but observers have largely focused on the oil factor. America uses up to 20 million barrels of oil a day. Bringing prices down, perhaps to below $20 levels, will certainly help. Since 1973, recessions had followed oil spikes in the U.S.. It is in the interest of the U.S. economy that the oil volatility is removed from the equation.

At the very least, oil spikes dampen consumer spending which accounts for 70 per cent of U.S.'s GDP. Going by this logic, the U.S. is understandably eager to prevent the use of oil as a weapon, a prospect that Saddam Hussein would have kept alive. Additionally, the U.S. will want Iraq to pump more than the pre-war levels of 1.8 million barrels a day. The international public opinion will judge the veracity of the American assertion that securing the oil fields was for the strategic interests of Iraqis. It is beguiling that the plight of Iraqis should stir passions in Washington, but not the future of Afghans—the first of the nations "softened" by American forces. Unlike Afghanistan, Iraqi oil can potentially at some point in the future, weaken the ability of OPEC to influence prices through its quota system. Iraq's oil reserves are second only to Saudi Arabia, a key member of OPEC, which sets out to keep prices within the range of $22 to $28 per barrel. For an idea of Iraq's strategic potential, Saudi produces 8 million barrels a day. A new oil map is being drawn.

The oil-equation analysis was mostly correct until the impasse at the U.N. Security Council which culminated in the U.S.-U.K. axis deciding to invade Iraq minus U.N. backing. Since then, the magnitude of the economic goal seems significantly much broader and more ambitious. It is about making Iraq the first oil economy managed and owned by the U.S.. This has led some commentators to even wonder if the U.S. was making a strategic business decision in snubbing the U.N. Remember that Russia and France have had a sizeable business interest in Iraqi oil. Will they be kept out now? "As occupying power," wrote Leon Fuerth, a former national security adviser to Al Gore, "the United States will unilaterally assume responsibility for decisions that will determine the future course of Iraq's oil and gas industries. We become in effect a virtual member of OPEC, and one of the most powerful at that. So, immense military power will be united with an equally impressive form of economic power."

The world is unnerved by the prospect. *The Economist* (March 22, 2003) referred to the "suspicions that the administration will hand out the most lucrative construction projects to American companies." Jay Garner, the retired general briefly made chief re-constructor of Iraq, heads SY Technology, a California-based missile defence specialist. *Financial Times* (April 4/5) said: "His company was acquired last year for $48 million by L-3 Communications, the tenth largest U.S. defence contractor. Guidance systems made by Mr. Garner's division are used in the type of missiles in the war on Iraq."

Analysts suggest the setting of the Iraqi Governing Council, unveiled on July 12, 2003, was a Public Relations exercise to show that the U.S. is not amassing power and riches. This notion has resulted in the incessant attacks the U.S. has had to endure in Iraq.

For now, the very public disagreements on the economic aspects of Iraq have died down. For Russian Foreign Minister Igor Ivanov had prior to this, agonised publicly that the U.S. might "freeze out Russia economically" from post-war Iraq. Lukoil of Russia has a big presence in Iraq, so were France's TotalFinaElf and the China National Petroleum Corp.

French companies, Alcatel, Peugeot, Renault and Schneider Electric were all doing business in Iraq. Will this change? America will be eager to douse the suspicion that it was out to colonise Iraq, but the domestic lobbies and realities may frustrate that public relations desire.

The others are unhappy. Russia's Igor Ivanov has said his country needed to protect its interests. Tony Blair said U.N. and not the U.S. should take charge of the re-construction of Iraq. This has been a key disagreement between the two close allies. Blair's failure to nudge Bush to reconsider will further diminish the standing of a once popular British Prime Minister seen to be fighting for his political life following his rigorous support for war.

Already we hear that the American "road map" for the reconstruction of Iraq outlines that State-owned companies will be privatised. It is anybody's guess as to who will actually own those big businesses. State-owned firms in the Middle East happen to be giant petrochemical firms.

Will Iraq and eventually the entire Middle East then be the new sources of American wealth, thus securing George Bush who grapples with a floundering economy, a brand new second term? Yes, with luck Iraqis will be gainfully employed. Should peace prevail and there is lasting stability, they will be better off. It does not obscure the fact that the world has been misled, because the biggest beneficiaries of post-war Iraq will be the Americans. I suppose American lobbies would have preferred that Washington keep out U.N. for as long as it could so that American businesses don't have to share the spoil. I have always argued that should American casualties mount, they would be forced to reconsider. By September 2003, *The Washington Post* reported that almost 10

American combatants a day were now being officially declared "wounded in action".

Iraq is left with one-tenth of its former riches because of the suffocating sanctions. Two millions Iraqis were visiting Europe each year before the sanctions were imposed! Long before 1991, a large number of foreigners were working in Iraq. Blair and the rest of the world are leery about having U.S. dictates post-war Iraq. Some including Iraqi opposition, are against idea of the occupying power running the country. Rashid Khalidi of University of Chicago's Centre for International Studies, said "Iraqi were the most avid readers in the Arab world and should be able to rebuild their country."

The Americans don't think so. They may occupy Iraq for years. U.S. accusers insist this is a premeditated grab, and the Bush Administration has a case to answer. Especially given the self-righteous posturing in the run-up to war. Bush was rapidly replacing the motivation for the invasion with a kinder excuse. But he would not let the weapons inspectors finish their task. It shows that the rhetoric about this being a war against terrorism, a bid to disarm Iraq, and in the final flourish, a desire to bring "freedom and prosperity", that this was about free nations of the world versus protector of terror, has been plainly all propaganda. According to Dan Plesch, a British defence analyst, the freedom and democracy talk "is a confidence trick designed to draw Western liberals into providing legitimacy for an old-fashioned conquest."

At the outset of the invasion, protesters in Moscow brought containers of oil to the residence of the U.S. Ambassador and said: "Please take this oil and stop the war." I join others in being sceptical about the intentions of Washington and the future of Iraq. In retrospect, all that mattered was the

U.S. war timetable. When told that Saddam Hussein was complying with Resolution 1441, Bush saw it as a "willful charade." "Why a little more time, when Saddam has had 12 years to disarm!" he thundered. Once they were ready for war, they simply ditched the U.N. Privately, the Bush Administration officials are worried of the repercussions on its image from the failure to discover any trace of weapons of mass destruction so far. "The president has made very clear that the reason why we are in Iraq is to find weapons of mass destruction," Assistant Secretary of State for Nonproliferation, John Wolf, told MSNBC News. "Very clearly, we need to find this stuff or people are going to ask questions." Given that the U.S. insisted vehemently that Saddam be de-fanged, the failure will manifest a doubly wicked ploy. That, they were all the while scheming, hoping to attack a toothless Iraq. Intriguingly, the focus has also quickly turned to the "potentially costly contracts" of destroying the banned substances if they are indeed discovered. One company in the running for the contracts is of course Halliburton's KBR.

Donald Rumsfeld, was initially blamed for insisting on a lean force to invade Iraq, but the 250,000-strong force was not very much inferior in size to the Iraqi Army, and this has been a war, as Paul Krugman put it, between the U.S. that has an annual military budget of $400 billion and Iraq a nation that spends $1.4 billion on military. And, one that has been significantly weakened.

Conquest is a natural consequence of pursuing business interests through war. Iraqis are acutely aware that conquests never bring freedom. Some Iraqis may admittedly be terrified of the Saddam regime but this is a question of national survival. The wrong assumptions that Iraqis would have lined the streets to greet the invaders will return to haunt

Rumsfeld, Cheney and others, as historians dissect their convictions and war strategies.

Soon, the Americans will return to the drawing board knowing that Iraq's neighbours will be in perpetual stupor. Egypt gets $3 billion annually in U.S. aid and another $1 billion in "gifts". Jordan gets $1 billion. Turkey was hoping to let U.S. troops run over Iraq via its soil for a $26 billion-bounty. I have said it and will say it again—the Arabs will have to get out of the present morass through hard work and by being united. Against the overpowering commercial and strategic interests of the U.S., they don't have a chance.

The very first task of the U.S. Military on descending on Iraqi shores was to protect the oil fields. The politics of oil soon unfolded forcing Russia and France to backpedal.

Will the U.S.-occupied Iraq try to pump as much oil as possible, thus shattering the sacrosanct quota system of OPEC?

The quota is set by OPEC, which is helmed by Saudi Arabia, to influence prices. OPEC producers would boost production as they did before U.S. invaded Iraq as they thought the conflict might trigger "shortages and soaring prices, that could hurt the economies of their best consumers".[1] Likewise OPEC producers would be anxious to cut quotas to halt falling prices. Iraq has always been somewhat of a loose cannon in the oil equation. Under Saddam it had on occasions called for oil embargo to hurt the U.S., which imports 60 per cent of its oil consumption. Worse, Saddam wanted to trade in Euro, not the U.S. dollar.

---

1 "Refining OPEC's Quotas—Facing Oversupply, Cartel to Weigh Production Cuts", *The Washington Post*, April 23, 2003

The Iraqi bellicose was watched with much foreboding by the U.S. as uncertainties would push up prices and hurt the U.S. economy. A $1 increase in oil prices means adding an extra $20 million to its costs per day. A drop in prices would be a wonderful bonus to the U.S. economy.

By sharp contrast, Russia and Saudi Arabia, among others, will be hurt by low prices. Russia's oil output might even pip the Saudi production of 8 million barrels a day. A $1 increase in oil prices put an extra $1 billion into the Russian state budget.[2] Iraq under normal circumstances is the world's eighth largest oil producer, with access to 112 billion of proven oil reserves. Only Saudi has more reserves at 262 billion barrels. Before the war, Iraq was producing about 2.5 million barrels a day, some 2 million of which were exported under U.N. supervision through the "oil-for-food" programme in place since 1996. Since its inception, the programme has overseen more than $100 billion in contracts for oil exports and relief imports combined.[3]

With 13 million barrels of oil passing though the Persian Gulf each day, the region is of strategic interest to the U.S.. And, it continuously seeks to secure reliable sources of oil supply. Its foreign dependence is rising, and expected to reach 70 per cent by the year 2010. The U.S. is also scrambling for oil in West Africa and the Caspian Sea but as many commentators had argued Iraq "has become the linchpin in a U.S. strategy to secure cheap oil while breaking the clout of the Arab-dominated oil cartel, OPEC."[4]

---

2 David G. Victor and Nadejda M. Victor, "Axis of Oil?", *Foreign Affairs*, Mar./Apr. 2003

3 "Oil, Food and a Whole Lot of Questions", *New York Times*, Apr. 18, 2003

4 Lutz C. Kleveman, "The new 'Great Game' being played out over oil," *The Independent*, Mar. 31, 2003

The conduct of the U.S. since it started beating the war drums on Iraq had been predictable. Remember the "No blood for oil" bellowed by the anti-war protesters as Tony Blair famously insisted on March 7, 2003 that "we don't touch it (Iraqi oil), and the U.S. doesn't touch it"?

When the U.S. forces moved into Baghdad in early April 2003, they let looters terrorise the city. The Oil Ministry was under round-the-clock surveillance with every entrance blocked by 50 U.S. tanks. In the early days of the invasion, U.S. troops rushed to secure the oil fields. Washington faced the embarrassing revelations that oil contracts, starting with the fighting of oil fires, were being quickly dished out to cronies.

As quickly Washington denied that Halliburton would be a major player. However, *The Guardian*[5] reported on May 8 that Halliburton has a bigger role than previously admitted and that it was already operating oil fields in the country through its subsidiary, KBR. A *Forbes* (July 21, 2003) article reported that KBR engineering unit has a team of 50 engineers working seven days a week in Iraq rebuilding its oil infrastructure. However, the Iraqi technocrats are taking charge of reconstruction, and they don't need the new technology being offered by the Americans.

While it is true that it will take U.S. and Iraq years to pump up to six, seven million barrels a day, secured Iraqi oil fields would moderate prices. Also, the U.S. and Britain, acknowledging that they are occupying powers of Iraq, now have absolute control over Iraq's oil revenues.

---

5 In March 2003, *The Guardian* reported that Cheney was still receiving annual payments of up to $1 million from Halliburton, in the form of "deferred compensation" from his golden handshake.

Additionally, U.S. companies led by ExxonMobil would be in the running for the privatisation of Iraqi oil. Interestingly, the oil equation has complicated the bid by U.S.-U.K. to lift sanctions they had imposed on Iraq. Russia resisted for some weeks before giving in. After all, Russia's Lukoil was given by Saddam the contract to develop the eight billion barrel West Qurna oil field. France's TotalFinaElf has an interest in Majnoon and Bin Umar oil fields. Who will be getting these lucrative contracts?

The man acting as liaison between Paul Bremer and acting oil minister, Thamir Ghadbhan, is Phillip Carrol, former head of Royal Dutch Shell's U.S. operation. Now Adviser to Iraq's Ministry of Oil, he told *The Washington Post* in May 2003 that it might be in "Iraq's interest to disregard quotas set by OPEC and export as much oil as it can."

Phillip Carrol had since admitted that he owns substantial shares in Shell. Will Iraq now leave OPEC? Former Iraqi Oil Minister Fadhil Chalabi said indeed this would be the case, as Iraq would need much more than the output allocated to it by OPEC to revive its ruined economy.

The upshot of it all is Iraqis will lose control of their oil assets under the guise of privatisation, certain to benefit the American and British companies.

If oil is the primary motivation, I have been asked, why Americans have not invaded Nigeria or something when West Africa's share in U.S. oil import is expected to rise to 25 per cent by 2015? It is simple. American Jews are anxious that Israel gets maximum protection. The July 2003 visit by President George Bush to key African nations including Nigeria does indicate the West Africa's growing importance as an oil supplier to the U.S.—especially when it is half the distance to refineries on East Coast of America, compared to supplies from the Persian Gulf. African oil now provides 15 per cent of American imports.

Chapter 8

THE MEDIA BATTLE

> "Lying is central to the survival of nations and to the success of great enterprises, because if our enemies can count on the reliability of everything you say, your vulnerability is enormously increased .... Look at the map of the world: national boundaries have not been drawn by peaceful men leading lives of spiritual contemplation. National boundaries have been established by war, and national character has been shaped by struggle, most often bloody struggle."
>
> *Michael Ledeen*,
> American Enterprise Institute

NINE-ELEVEN has overnight changed the tone of the debate on freedom of the Press. It has robbed the U.S. of a powerful leverage. By exposing the deep chasm between the liberal and the right-wing Press in the U.S., Nine-eleven has liberated the media in the poorer countries. Through their own coverage of the Iraq War, the American Press has made the poorly funded newspapers around the world look superior. I sat in many UMNO Supreme Council Press conferences where reporters asked tougher questions than the White House press corps dare quiz George Bush. The Malaysian Press can do with more in-depth reports because by the time our newspapers are delivered, we have been bombarded with endless news nuggets. Otherwise, I say the Malaysian media should not be apologetic over their stances and views.

Here's why:

Rupert Murdoch and the hawks in Washington think CNN is too liberal. Newt Gingrich, the former Speaker of the House of Representatives, mockingly call it Clinton News Network. Fox News espouses unabashedly pro-American views. A Fox anchor described France as a member of the "Axis of Weasels". After Nine-eleven, Geraldo Rivera, Fox News war correspondent, armed himself with a pistol and proclaimed that he would be honoured to kill Osama bin Laden.[1] Al Gore described Fox, owned by Murdoch's News Corp, as "a virtual arm of the Republican Party".

Malaysians have had precious perspectives since Nine-eleven watching those American, British, Arabic, German and Chinese news networks.

Al-Jazeera has announced plans to start an English news network in 2004. Already we are inundated with new private and Government-funded Arabic news networks. There are 30-odd Arabic channels with Arab journalists criticising state policies, attacking corruption and pushing for social and political change. The Arab satellite stations are distrusted by Arab regimes and by members of the Iraqi Governing Council. *Al-Jazeera* previously praised by the U.S., has had run-ins with Arab regimes and with the American occupiers in Iraq. Paul Wolfowitz told Fox News that *Al-Jazeera* was "inciting violence" and "endangering the lives of American troops".

---

1 The American media credo since Nine-eleven seems to be "be fair, be accurate and be American."

Saddam was unpleasant to media critics. His last Information Minister Mohamed Saeed As-Sahaf, according to *Al-Jazeera* Baghdad's bureau chief, Wadah Khanfar, physically assaulted *Al-Jazeera* reporters.

Al-Jazeera is still treated badly now that Saddam has gone. Its offices and staff "have been subject to strafing by gunfire, death threats, confiscation of news material, multiple detentions and arrests, all carried out by U.S. soldiers." So said, Wadah Khanfar.

As an occupier, Washington is a media buster; as a promoter of democracy it insists on freedom of the Press. In Iran, Washington is funding media operations to promote "freedom and democracy". Should Iran replace the clergy-rule with an American-friendly regime, they will come down hard on the media in the name of stability. I suggest that the International Federation of Journalists and Commonwealth Press Union investigate charges of lack of Press freedom in Iraq.

The Malaysian Press was previously described as "slavishly compliant" making the country "an illiberal democracy". I suggest that Malaysian newspapers discuss media issues. Explain your own ideals and convictions to your readers. Then they will understand your thinking better and will decide whether or not they should read your newspaper. Give Malaysians space to praise or thump you. When *The New York Times* executive editor Howell Raines and its managing editor Gerald M. Boyd had to step down over the Jayson Blair affair,[2] a major debate ensued.

---

2 In the first two years of his career since joining *The New York Times* in 1999, he piled up 50 corrections. While sitting in his apartment, he filed stories from 20 cities. He has since produced a book proposal with "I really screwed up" as the starting line.

We see similar self-analysis in the British Press about them. The BBC is funded by the British Government, which redirects fees paid by television owners to the public broadcaster. The Charter is to end year 2006. The BBC prides itself in being impartial, perpetually suspected by both the Labour Party and the Conservatives Party of favouring the other.

The BBC has been in the news since the Iraq War following a series of exposes that alarmed the British Government including allegations that Downing Street had sexed up the dossier on Iraq's Weapons of Mass Destruction. The BBC is barred from Zimbabwe and now covers the African country from South Africa. The BBC's documentary on Israel's nuclear weapons programme drew charges of the BBC being anti-Semitic. Israel increasingly favours Fox News, owned by Rupert Murdoch.

The British Government is alleged to have tried to muscle in on the BBC including issuing veiled threats concerning the BBC Charter. I have been following the developments of the British media and politics for 40 years now. I notice that this is a rare occasion for the liberal and right-wing media to be united in opposing the Downing Street over its attacks on the BBC.

There is a distinct right-wing Press in the British Media, *The Daily Telegraph* and *The Daily Mail*, the latter critics suggest, still thinks there is a British Empire out there. Their reporters and columnists don't seem able to agree on anything. The liberal media has been generally against the Iraq War and critical of the American treatment of those Afghan's unlawful combatants being held under harsh conditions in Guantánamo Bay. The American Press curiously does not think that merits a mention.

Fox News took a hard pro-American line throughout the War, a move that saw its ratings soared. The BBC has more finesse and depth, with 250 correspondents.

I hope despite the end of major combat operations in Iraq, Malaysians will stay tuned to the events unfolding and to follow them with an analytical mind. Study the verbal acrobatics being performed by the war advocates. Analyse their media. This is an opportunity to grasp American policy on the Middle East, the humiliation of occupation first suffered by Palestinians, and now conceivably Iraqis too and the Israeli hegemony in the Middle East. I am sure we are all developing a big appetite for knowledge.

I have been asked: "Who are these neo-cons?" I found the BBC's *Panorama* ran in May 2003 on the subject most startling. It shows how the neo-cons so willfully run American foreign policy.

Their bitterest critics say neo-cons are all Jews. Some of the ranking neo-cons like Paul Wolfowitz detest the labeling. Others like Richard Perle (called Prince of Darkness over his hardline anti-Soviet stance) seems to relish the label. Perle told *Panaroma* that the Holocaust was a defining moment in the shaping of the American foreign policy!

Note that the neo-cons use the media effectively to advance their cause. They give endless briefings to the media. In the op-ed pages of *The Washington Post* and *The Wall Street Journal*, the neo-cons have found prized allies. These two opinion leaders are unwavering supporters of President Bush's foreign policy—that is the invasion of Iraq, which in turn was influenced by the neo-cons.

Prof. Elliot Cohen, yet another neo-con member of the Defense Policy Board, called the fight against so-called Islamic extremists, terrorism and rogue regimes (translated as Islam) as the Fourth World War (the Cold War was third). Cohen will always be given space in the op-ed pages of *The Wall Street Journal* to defend and justify his radical ideas; and the likes of Robert Kagan[3] and James Woolsey,[4] formerly CIA director, will rush to back the idea in those same op-ed pages. Woolsey wrote in *The Wall Street Journal* in April 2003: "Victory in this world war (IV) will depend not only on U.S. skill in battle and effectiveness in rolling up terrorist cells. It will depend on America being able to split as many potential adherents as possible away from its many totalitarian enemies: Sunni Islamists (al-Qaeda, its fellow travellers/financiers), Shite Islamists (Tehran's *mullahs*, Hezbollah), and Syria, Libya and Sudan (each with a somewhat different ideological cover story to justify oppression)." I find such language deeply offensive. We must crush such arguments by rebutting their wicked claims. These are the ideologues trying relentlessly to smear the Muslim World and impose their values.

In case the guest writers are unable to counter their opponents, the editorial writers of *The Wall Street Journal* will wade in. This was from the April 17-20, 2003 edition: "But the majority of the American left, and especially its leading media voices, remain flummoxed if not embarrassed by America's Iraq victory. These include most Democrats in Congress, the editors (though not all reporters) of the *New*

---

3 Robert Kagan wrote the much-talked-about "Power and Weakness" essay. He is a leading neo-con.

4 Woolsey, like Prof. Elliot Cohen, is a key member of the Defense Policy Board.

York Times[5] and its acolytes at CNN and the major networks, and of course most academic experts."

Is that so? Writing in *Foreign Affairs*, Richard Lambert, who was formerly editor of the *Financial Times*, said: "In the United States, it is rare to come across strong opposition to Bush's policies in the mainstream media outside the op-ed pages of *The New York Times*."

The New York Times is certainly not hostile to Israel. It once had a policy of not sending a Jew correspondent to Tel Aviv and its first Jewish correspondent in Israel, Thomas Friedman, is a supporter of the invasion of Iraq. To antiwar protests of No Blood for Oil!, he said: "Why Not?". Friedman described the setting up of the governing council as "the most important day in its modern history."

In case anyone doubted his commitment to Israel, Friedman wrote earlier: "This President Bush—Dubya—if he keeps going in the direction he's been going, will be remembered as the president who got so wrapped around the finger of Ariel Sharon that he indulged Israel into thinking it really could have it all—settlements, prosperity, peace and democracy—and in doing so helped contribute to the slow erosion of the Jewish state."

The challenge is to get the mainstream Arab views into the American media. The late Edward Said and gang are operating very much on the periphery, through obscure medium like the *IslamOnLine* and *Counterpunch*.

The Wall Street Journal and their conservative brethrens are unable to fathom the rest of the world's concern over the distinctly pro-Israel stance of Washington. Lambert said Euro-

---

5 *New York Times* columnist Maureen Dowd routinely exposes the neo-cons.

peans see the Bush Administration as captive of the Israel lobby and the Christian lobby.

In case *The Wall Street Journal* lacks firepower, their trans-Atlantic colleagues, opinion writers at London's *The Daily Telegraph* will be asked to write for the *Journal*.

London's *Independent* (set up by former editorial writers of *The Daily Telegraph*) and *The Guardian* are staunchly anti-Iraq war and had carried numerous articles exposing the neo-con's motives, and the riches some of its leading members had acquired.

The Sunday newspaper, *The Observer*, revealed on May 11, 2003 that James Woolsey is a "director of a U.S. firm aiming to make millions of dollars from 'the war on terror'. Woolsey is a director of private equity firm Paladin Capital set up in the aftermath of Nine-eleven offering "substantial promise for homeland security investment". The firm believes in the U.S. Government will in the next few years spend $60 billion on anti-terrorism that would not have been spent before Nine-eleven. In 2001, Paul Wolfowitz assigned Woolsey to Europe to argue the case for links between Saddam Hussein and al-Qaeda.

In fact according to the American watchdog, the Center for Public Integrity, nine members of the Defense Policy Board, have ties to defence contractors that won more than $76 billion in defence contracts in 2001 and 2002.

The likes of Woosley are undeterred by the mounting criticisms leveled against the Bush Administration's policy on Iraq. He appeared on BBC's *HARDtalk* in July 2003 to deflect some of the criticisms and maintain their anti-Saddam line.

We should take note of the bombings of *Al-Jazeera*'s offices in Kabul and Baghdad, preceded by the bombing of

Belgrade TV Station by NATO Forces. Bill Clinton and Tony Blair had at that time, said the bombing was "in response to a deliberate misinformation campaign being carried out by Belgrade TV." Now Arab journalists believe the destruction of *Al-Jazeera* office in Baghdad was designed to "remove the witnesses" from the horrible war.

Al-Jazeera's Tariq Ayoub, a Spanish and *Reuters*[6] cameramen all died within hours of each other, as U.S. forces attacked in quick succession the clearly-marked *Al-Jazeera* office in a residential area, the office of Abu Dhabi Television and the Palestine hotel where most foreign journalists were based.

I saw an NBC correspondent at Pentagon suggesting that Tariq could have been targeted by the Iraqis to prevent *Al-Jazeera* from reporting the death of Saddam Hussein. Given *Al-Jazeera*'s credibility among the Arabs, the Pentagon correspondent reasoned, the Arabs would believe that Saddam is dead should *Al-Jazeera* report it.

The Palestine Hotel was attacked by tank fire as a response to what was thought to be sniping coming from hotel. Yet all the journalists at the hotel did not hear any shot coming from the hotel. Many now believe the American troops must have mistaken a camera to be a dangerous weapon.

Is this an American message to the journalists? I wish to refer readers to President Bush's speech hours before the war began when he pointedly advised journalists to leave Iraq.

---

6 On Aug. 17, 2003, an American tank shot dead another Reuters cameraman, Mazen Dana, while he was filming near a U.S.-run prison on the outskirts of Baghdad.

Were they planning to unleash a cruel attack to instill fear in the minds of Iraqis and "enemies" elsewhere?

Ominously *Al-Jazeera* office in Kabul was also attacked during the Afghan campaign. These are the days of "the embeds" and sanitising war with *The New York Times* branding this as showing "carnage with a soft-focus lens".

Bucking the trend was *Al-Jazeera*, earning it vilification by London and Washington for practising the same Press freedom they preach on others. President Bush talks about free nations and Prime Minister Blair spins the yarns about Iraqis being free to speak their mind. *Al-Jazeera* was condemned for telling the truth.

Since they were no embeds on the Iraqi side, there was no media images of the Iraqi forces. They were invisible.

Robert Keeble, a professor of journalism at Lincoln University, wrote that reporters "who dared to operate away from the pools, were intimidated by the military and some of their journalistic colleagues."[7] Peter Arnett of the Gulf War fame was sacked by NBC for speaking his mind in an interview with Iraqi TV.

Someone said compelling reporters to stick with the U.S.-U.K. troops meant "killing the media by kindness." And I say manipulating the media would leave the permanent danger of the world presuming that modern warfare is relatively safe and clean; thus aggressors can go on and attack other countries.

Through embedded reporters and the desire of the media to sanitise war, the otherwise gruesome wars are reduced to awesome television show of tactical ingenuity and over-

---

7 *The Independent*, March 31, 2003

whelming firepower. It is not about deaths and sufferings anymore. When *Al-Jazeera* showed civilian casualties, the so-called "free nations" denounced it as "emotive Arab propaganda aimed at orchestrating hostilities towards the Allies". The Americans were watching war-entertainment on TV and as more Iraqis are slaughtered, support for war in the U.S. grows.

At 10 deaths, more journalists died in Iraq than in any recent conflicts. With the exception of David Bloom of NBC who died of natural causes, the others were non-embeds. Geoff Hoon, the British Defence Secretary, said the embedded programme was in part to protect journalists and "it's also good for people watching". Jack Straw, his British Cabinet colleague, suggested that the Allied would not have won World War II if 24-hour satellite television was covering the war.

In Iraq, journalists openly said they had to take sides to cover the war properly, but Western journalism gurus unfailingly tell reporters from the Third World that their brand of journalism is wrong. Journalism is about reporting things that go wrong, they thundered. How wrong can the marauding troops possibly be when journalists were permanently embedded with the U.S. military? High visibility journalists sound suspiciously as spokesmen of the U.S. military. The journalism manuals should now be revised to include this qualifier: "During a crisis, rally around the flag and improve the news!"

The White House's Office of Global Communications that ran the media strategy made sure the American journalists behave; 700 were sent in as embeds. ABC's Ted Koppel, embedded with the 3rd Infantry Division, when asked on war progress, said:

"Let's be perfectly candid about this. We get much of our news either when we chat with you or when we listen ... to the BBC on shortwave on the hour."

Chapter 9

IMPERIAL AMERICA

> "The Plan is for the United States to rule the world. The overt theme is unilateralism, but it is ultimately a story of domination. It calls for the United States to maintain its overwhelming military superiority and prevent new rivals from rising up to challenge it on the world stage. It calls for dominion over friends and enemies alike. It says not that the United States must be more powerful, or most powerful, but that it must be absolutely powerful."
>
> *David Armstrong*

> "I think all foreigners should stop interfering in the internal affairs of Iraq."
>
> *Paul Wolfowitz*, while touring American-occupied Iraq in July 2003

AMERICA now rules Iraq. This was emphasised by George E. Irani, of Royal Roads University (Canada). Writing in the Lebanese-based *Daily Star Online*, he proclaimed: "The Arab League has a new unofficial member, the United States of America".

The limited powers of the Iraqi Governing Council underline the pecking order in Iraq, as to who actually rules the country. The Council can appoint diplomats but not Ambassadors. The Council can appoint Ministers and 25 were actually appointed subsequently, but not to defence and security posts. Whatever they do, the U.S.-led Coalition Provincial Authority headed by Paul Bremer, can veto them. Of the 25 members, 16 were either in exile or from Kurdish self-rule areas.

To many observers, the Iraqi adventure exposes America's imperialistic tendencies, a penchant which some think is necessary to keep the peace around the world. This debate rages on. For a debate to rage, there has to be opposing sides and competing interests. So, we hear of such terms as "assertive nationalists", "democratic imperialists', "neo-conservatives" and "neo-liberals". I am sure the phraseology will expand.

Despite what the differing bodies of opinions in the U.S. say or do, America is already organising the world system to suit its interests. There seems to be a unity of purpose. Control over oil resources is a key strategy, a pattern pronounced in Iraq where the twin occupiers, the U.S. and Britain, have absolute control over oil.

Iraq is the first project of the Bush Doctrine that authorises the U.S. to execute regime changes unilaterally. By comparison, it surpasses the arrogance level of Monroe Doctrine that proclaimed America's right to intervene in Latin America to prevent European powers from doing so.

As a hyper-power, the U.S. might have found its might to be inadequate. For, unlike the British Empire, the U.S. had been without a direct control over other sovereign countries. Until its forces arrived in Iraq, that is. Iraq under America may well recognise Israel, thus dramatically altering balances in the region and further complicating the elusive Arab unity.

The British historian Niall Ferguson regards the U.S. as an "empire in denial". Indeed the likes of Donald Rumsfeld has doggedly denied that the U.S. is imperialistic. George Monbiot, author of *Poisoned Arrows* and *No Man's Land*, said the U.S. is no longer just a nation. "It is now a religion ... they are no longer simply killing enemies; they are casting out demons. The people who reconstructed the faces of Uday and Qusay Hussein carelessly forgot to restore the pair of little horns on each brow." How the U.S. flexes its muscle from now on and tolerate international dissent will shape events around the world.

Funnily enough, *Washington Post* columnist Michael Kelly said the U.S. "seeks not to own foreign land but to make the world behave better—indeed be better."

One assertion, about land ownership is simply wrong. America had displayed an imperialistic streak from early on—from 1857 when its troops were first stationed in Panama. Encouraged, the U.S. in 1898 took the Philippines but lost 4,273 soldiers. Its other colonial wars proved to be a breeze. In Haiti (1915-1920), 146 U.S. soldiers died; in Dominican Republic (1916-1922, 144 dead) and in Nicaragua (1927-1932, 136 dead). In 1904 a year after Panama declared its Independence, America signed a treaty with Panama that "granted" rights to the U.S. as if it were sovereign in zone roughly 10 miles wide and 50 miles long. In that the U.S. would build a canal then administer, fortify and defend it. In 1989, Bush Sr. dispatched American troops to Panama to "protect U.S. lives and property, to fulfill U.S. Treaty responsibilities to operate and defend the Canal and assist the Panamanian people in restoring democracy and to bring Manuel Noriega to justice." The U.S. did return the Canal to Panama in 1999 while keeping the Guantánamo Bay in Cuba where the al-Qaeda prisoners are now being held.

The other Michael Kelly contention about policing behaviour is ominous. It strikes at the heart of the anxieties of the rest of the world. What worries us all is America will become a permanent bully. To quote political theorist Yaron

Ezrahi, "they project an arrogance and obsession with power alone."

We have witnessed displays of might. On November 3, 2002, a rocket attack on a car in Yemen liquidated six people, suspected to be al-Qaeda members. According to a *Reuters* report, Yemen authorities would not say the cause of the car blast but Paul Wolfowitz told CNN: "One hopes each time you get a success like that, not only to have gotten rid of somebody dangerous, but to have imposed changes in their tactics and operations." One of the dead is said to be Qaed Senyan al-Harthi, a suspect in the 2000 bombing of the USS destroyer USS *Code* in Aden, which killed 17 U.S. sailors. Do the Bush Doctrine and the pre-emption policy mean anyone can be attacked anytime without the burden of proof and without trial?

Indeed the conduct of the leader of the imperialistic power will be closely watched. Polly Toynbee, a columnist for *The Guardian* thought she saw a new-age Emperor when Bush addressed the U.N. in 2002. "There he stood, this unlikely Emperor of the world, telling U.N.'s 190 nations how it is going to be," she observed.[1]

Even if Bush is not imperialistic, he is surrounded by a cabal devoted to coercive democratisation in pushing for democracy in the Middle East. While this is patronising, the attitude is unlikely to change because the U.S. is getting mightier.

"The new Rome meets the new barbarians," said the March 23, 2002 issue of the *The Economist* by way of introducing a piece by Joseph Nye, Dean of Harvard University's John F. Kennedy of School of Government and author of *The*

---

[1] Polly Toynbee, "The Last Emperor", *The Guardian*, Sept. 13, 2002

Paradox of American Power: Why the World's Only Superpower Can't Go It Alone.

Trouble is, America's might is far from diminishing. It spends more militarily than those of the next eight countries combined. America has a 31 per cent share of world product, equal to the combined share of Japan, Germany, Britain and France. Rabid Tabbarah, director of the Center for Development Studies and Projects in Beirut, said: "Many in the developing world hate the U.S. because they feel military threatened by it." The Project for the New American Century formed by key members of the Bush Administration when they were outside the Government, argued for permanent U.S. bases in Saudi Arabia and Kuwait and even a regime change in China and increased military presence in South East Asia.

Jay Bookman of the *Atlanta-Journal Constitution* has been among those who believes U.S. will create permanent military bases in Iraq from which "to dominate the Middle East, including neighbouring Iran."

And America is poised to produce a much bigger population than Europe by 2050, 550 million Americans to 360 million reversing present trends.[2] Europe is now more heavily populated than America's present total of 281 million but a big rise in fertility rate since the 1980s will change the equation significantly. Unlike the population of China and India, we are talking about half a billion affluent Americans. Culturally, the American values have been embraced by the world. The Arab Street may despise America for flexing its muscle but all the same the Arabs love everything American. At best the Arabs are torn between their passion for Ameri-

---

2 *The Economist*, "A Tale of Two Bellies", Aug. 24, 2002

can culture and their nationalistic fervour. Further, the Americans work harder than the Europeans. Americans take an average of 14 days of holiday a year compared to Italians (42 days), French (37) and Germans (35).

The Germans and the French opposed the war in Iraq and have been "snubbed" for their troubles. The leaders of Australia, Britain and Spain were rewarded with invitations to the Bush ranch to show Washington's appreciation at their support for the war. The French especially are still being punished for their "indiscretion". Less American tourists are heading for France. America markets democracy but is not being very democratic.

That has not stopped the Americans from arguing with convictions about wanting to democratise the Arab World. Funnily enough, Turkey was penalised for upholding democracy. Turkey put the issue of allowing American forces passage to invade Iraq to a vote and was defeated. As a result it was penalised. The American military forces are being rushed to former Russian satellites. Qatar is being rewarded and the Saudis punished. The U.S. prefers a democratic Iraq to be secular but how could it ignore the considerable influence wielded by the Shia clerics?

There are roughly 15 million Shia Muslims in Iraq. The seminary or *hazwa* in Najaf is headed by four senior *ayatollahs*. In 1980, Ayatollah Muhammad Baqr al-Sadr was executed in al-Sadr City, allegedly by Saddam. Nineteen years later, another al-Sadr scion, Grand Ayatollah Sadiq al-Sadr was murdered with his two sons on a road near Najaf. "Shias from Beirut to Tehran marched in the streets denouncing Saddam."[3] The BBC reported then that the murder sparked riot-

---

3 Frank Smyth, *American Prospect Online*, Mar. 25, 2002

ing and clashes between Government forces and Shia Muslims.

Now, did Saddam really kill those *ayatollahs*? Did he, after being deposed, also planned the murder of Ayatollah Mohamed Baqir al-Hakim in a car bomb in late August 2003 that also killed 100 others?

The Americans will have to find the answers and also find a way to work with those *ayatollahs* unwilling to cooperate with them, or betray the very democratic principles they espouse. They cannot tell Iraqis not to vote for unfriendly *ayatollahs*, in the same manner as those *ayatollahs* cannot be urging Americans against voting for the right-wingers.

Donald Rumsfeld talks about democracy but had warned from the outset that the *mullahs* must not come into power.

The Arabs meanwhile have brought the devastating defeat in Iraq upon themselves. Some are assisting U.S. to reconfigure balance of power. U.S. and Israel are firmly in driver's seat as some Arab power sulk away or fear Arab Street backlash.

Is the U.S. close to ditching the Saudis? It is already embracing the new Iraq and a clutch of Gulf States. Emir of Qatar was in U.S. Major U.S. base is already in Qatar. American troops in Saudi had been moved to Qatar. Will the House of Saud fall? Has Egypt outlived its usefulness as a major political force in the region? And, democracy and regime change in Syria?

In Iraq, worst-case scenarios may still explode that could further fuel anti-Americanism sentiments. The tormented people of Iraq may turn more strident in demanding that the U.S. forces leave, and this uprising could be brutally met. Writing in the *Financial Times* (July 13, 2003) Douglas Hurd, the former British Foreign Secretary wondered if Fallujah is particularly hostile because it was a Baathist stronghold or "because during two days in May, U.S. troops shot down at least 16 people in its streets?"

In any case, anti-Americanism will fester. Before the war, Al-Qtaiba Rowda, 22, a United Arab Emirates University student who speaks fluent English, told an American journalist: "It seems America always needs an enemy. Now Islam is the enemy."[4]

The Americans may want to consider self-analysis, rather than keep on blaming others. An analysis by Barry Rubib, director of the Global Research in International Affairs Centre in an essay called *"Real Roots of Arab Anti-Americanism"*[5] sums up the prevalent attitude of the U.S.

He unreservedly absolves the United States from fault lines in Arab politics, claiming that Arab sentiments were emboldened by the perceived softness of the U.S. and Arab anti-Americanism is grounded in domestic maneuvering of groups fanning anti-U.S. feelings to distract public attention. He said the U.S. has a pro-Arab policy. "Since the pro-Shah Iranian coup of 1953, there has not been a single use of U.S. covert intervention to change a Middle East regime. Only in Iraq has the U.S. made an attempt to overthrow a Government and so far not very effectively."

Such views prompted Zbigniew Brzezinski, National Security Adviser in the Carter Administration, to fire a spirited letter to the media.

---

4 "In Search for Democracy, U.S. is Rejected as a Guide", *New York Times*, Sept. 24, 2002

5 *Foreign Affairs*, Nov./Dec. 2002

Brzezinski, putting things in perspective, said: "... some supporters of the administration have been less careful ... arguing that Islamic culture in general is so hostile to the West, and especially to democracy, that it has created a fertile soil for terrorist hatred of America."

"Missing from much of the public debate is discussion of the simple fact that lurks behind every terrorist act is a specific political antecedent. That does not justify either the perpetrator or his political cause. Nonetheless, the fact is that almost all-terrorist activity originates from some political conflict and is sustained by it as well. That is true of the Irish Republican Army in Northern Ireland, the Basques in Spain, the Palestinians in the West Bank and Gaza, the Muslims in Kashmir and so forth."[6] Colin Powell too had been arguing that the causes of terrorism had to be found until he was compelled (perhaps) by politics to sound hawkish.

The behaviour of Arab rulers, meanwhile, adds to the confusion. They were glad to see the back of Saddam, and they had been working feverishly to achieve this. They pestered Bill Clinton to remove Saddam Hussein. A report revealed that Saudi Arabia was prepared to pay about $1 billion for the covert ouster of Saddam if the U.S. would match it. Saudi was prepared to pay more and in 1994 King Fahd had told Clinton that he had "rounded up support for the plan (ouster of Saddam) from Egypt, Jordan, Syria and even Iran." The Saudis balked when the U.S. counter proposed that each side contribute $20 million.[7]

Will the Middle East be any safer? Will an American-ruled Iraq pacify Israel now run by the likes of Ariel Sharon

---

6 Zbigniew Brzezinski, "Confronting Anti-American Grievances", *New York Times*, Sept. 1 2002

7 "The Prince," *The New Yorker*, Mar. 24, 2003

and the IDF chief of staff General Moshe Ya'alon who said their aim is to lead Palestinians to internalise "in the deepest recesses of their consciousness that they are a defeated people."[8]

New York Times's Thomas Friedman likes us to believe that the "progressive" Arabs back the Americans, but *Zogby International* released in October 2002 showed that "87 per cent of Saudis have an unfavourable view of the United States".[9]

At the outset I had a sense, and intriguingly so, the business of crushing Iraq was a camouflaged ploy to destablise Saudi Arabia. The House of Saud has enjoyed better treatment from the U.S. compared to the other Muslim countries because of the Saudi oil. In the 1980s, the U.S. dared to anger Israel by selling arms to Saudi.

Some of Saudi's policies are anomalous to the "democratic principles" championed by the U.S. Since Nine-eleven, the U.S. has been pressing the Saudis to crackdown on financiers of suspected terrorists. This will all change if the U.S. is no longer beholden to Saudi oil. Saudi will still sell its oil but the higher output will weigh down prices. America has already lined up alternative sources.

There had been well-publicised irritants and scowling encounters between these two allies. There was the killing of the 19 American servicemen in Saudi in 1996. America was none too pleased by a shift in Saudi oil policy after oil prices fell dramatically, down to $10 per barrel in 1998. Prices began rising in 1999 but Saudi production fell by a million bar-

---

8 *Financial Times*, Apr. 22, 2003 "Israel is an occupier with a duty to protect", by Hemry Siegman, a senior fellow at the Council of Foreign Relations.

9 Nicholas Kristof, "Stop looking at the Saudis as the enemy", *Business Times*, Oct. 24, 2002

rels per day. Crown Prince Abdullah met senior American oil executives in 1998 when he offered to re-open its oil sector to foreign companies but U.S.-Saudi relationship has soured markedly.

Politically, the U.S. will in the interim (until the new democracies start looking for masters and allies) be without major Muslim allies if it ditches Saudi and Egypt, thus further deepening the Clash of Civilisations. American interest in the Middle East will be reduced to one that is academic, weeding out yet-to-be defined terrorism and more cuddling of Israel.

Unsurprisingly, the U.S. seems irritated over suggestions that it has been after Iraqi oil, but the policy has not changed since Americans pushed hard for a stake in the nascent Arab oil industry in 1922. All empires devour some form of raw material.

Phillip Knightley, co-author of *The Secret Lives of Lawrence of Arabia*, said the break-up of the Arab State was at the behest of oil companies who "saw only too well that oil concessions and royalties would be easier to negotiate with a series of rival Arab States, lacking any sense of unity, than with a powerful independent Arab State in the Middle East." Knightley said in the distribution of the spoils, Sherif Hussein of Mecca "was offered 100,000 pound sterling a year not to make a nuisance of himself". This was to enable the Britain, France and the Americans to divide the oil wealth among them.

In a 1999 report, the National Security Council was unambiguous in articulating U.S.'s continued interest in the oil producing regions in ensuring its access to foreign oil.[10] In

---

[10] Nafeez Mosaddeq Ahmed, *The Great Deception*, Thinkers Library, Kuala Lumpur, 2002, contains a lot of little-known facts on the matter of American strategic interests.

fact in October 1999, the oil-rich region of Central Asia was reassigned by Pentagon to be under Florida-based U.S. Central Command, which already controls the U.S. forces in the Persian Gulf. Azerbaijan, Kazakhstan, Turkmenistan and Uzbekistan have oil and gas reserves worth an estimated $2.5 trillion to $3 trillion. There is now a possibility of the Central Command being moved permanently to Qatar.[11]

The Democratic Government who wrote the 1999 report has since been defeated. The Bush Administration understands oil politics better. Bush had in 1990 sold $848,000 worth of stock in Harken Energy two months before its value nose-dived. In fact, it was a subject of a Securities and Exchange Commission's (SEC) investigation.

Cheney authored *The U.S. National Energy Policy Report* that demanded a priority on easing U.S. access to Persian Gulf supplies.[12] "Washington's predatory interest in Iraqi oil is clear, whatever its political protestations about its motives for war," *The Observer* said.

Oil crucially influences economic growth. A $10 rise in the price of oil cuts more than 0.2 per cent of growth in America and Europe. Osama bin Laden's remarks that crude oil should sell at $144 per barrel have made the Bush Administration more jittery as anything above $30 per barrel will dent growth. The attack on the Limburg oil tanker off Yemen further unnerved the U.S. that forks out a lot of money to protect the oil reserves in the Middle East.

---

11 *Washingtonpost.com*, "U.S. Military Sending Command Staff to Gulf", Sept. 11, 2002

12 Ed Vulliamy, Paul Webster and Nick Panton Walsh, "Scramble to carve up Iraqi oil reserves lies behind U.S. diplomacy", *The Observer*, Oct. 6, 2002

America has seen an imminent threat to oil supply in the conduct of Iraq from the outset. After Iran nationalised its oil industry in 1953, Iraq did so in 1972 and Baghdad urged fellow Arabs to follow suit. Later, Saudi and Libya nationalised American stakes in oil companies. In April 2002, Saddam suspended oil exports for a month to protest Israeli invasion of the West Bank. There was talk that Iran and Libya—daily output of 3.5 million barrels—would support the move. Then there is Venezuela, the fourth largest exporter of oil and where President Hugo Chavez has emerged as a kingpin in the OPEC cartel. Supplier of 17 per cent of its oil import, the U.S. must have been worried at Chavez's gung-ho approach to oil prices.

America originally thought that the "reformed" Libya and Sudan whose cooperation in the war on terror had surprised Washington, would keep the oil supply flowing. A far better option is of course to secure Iraqi oil, and with the acquiescence of Russia, forms a new "Oil Axis"—Russia's 5 million barrels per day and Iraq's projected capacity of 4 million barrels could easily match Saudi's daily output of 8 million barrels.[13]

That four-fifths of the world's oil reserves are deposited in politically unstable areas make American quest for oil a protracted affair.

The raw material-angle is inadequate to wholly explain the imperialistic tendencies, characterised by the invasion of Iraq. There were other catalysts, not least the "behaviour" of Saddam Hussein.

---

[13] Michael T. Klare, *Foreign Affairs*, May/June 2002

Long before the Iraq War, Martin Woollacott wrote in *The Guardian*: "An Iraq war looms because a group of American conservatives, now very influential inside and outside this administration, came to the conclusion years ago that Saddam had challenged the U.S. and got away with it, and that his victory could not be allowed to stand."[14]

---

[14] Martin Woollacort, "Nothing and no one will stop this drift towards war", *The Guardian*, Oct. 4, 2002

Epilogue

"This administration, whose entry strategy was based on falsehood, with no exit strategy, has trapped our troops in Iraq and exposed them to greater harm."

Rep. Dennis Kucinich

IRONICALLY, the much-vaunted reconstruction of Iraq will now largely focus on the restoration of normalcy shattered by the very invasion. The invasion has unleashed forces previously shackled. This should not have come as a surprise. As "serial liberators", the British and then the Americans have been closely associated with Iraq.

Key institutions of the American system—the executive, business and media—have in a flash squandered their legitimacy to impose their will and so-called values on the rest of the world.

So comprehensive the spin and propaganda had been, this war business terrorised our consciousness. Day after day we are being cajoled to doubt our own sanity and to reconsider cherished values.

This mind game was fought with overwhelming ferocity that every pronouncement, every Press conference by Washington and London brought us discomfort. Facts and fallacies were neatly interwoven that the biggest "collateral damage"[1] has been truth and decency. Here's a catalogue:

1. Where is Saddam Hussein?

This is a man who gassed his own people, assassinated rivals, tortured dissidents and who is allegedly a potent threat to American interests. Why then, didn't such a brutal dictator unleash the cache of chemical and biological weapons in his possession on the invaders?

2. Target of Opportunity

This dreadful phrase refers to speculative shelling of targets thought to house senior Iraqi leaders, ideally, Saddam Hussein and his two sons. The first target of opportunity-hit occurred on the onset, after which the aggressors declared that Saddam and others could have been killed. Another horrendous hit came on the 20th day when the upper-middle-class Mansour neighbourhood was obliterated, smashed by four 2,000-pound (900kg) bombs. It seems that Saddam

[1] I would describe "collateral damage" as a euphemism for killings and civilian deaths invented by the Americans to make the war less vicious and gory. This is commonly described as a means to sanitise war. The latest war is littered with euphemisms. Embedded reporters sound like incarcerated journalists who see no other truths besides those sanctioned by the invading force. Arundhati Roy, the brilliant writer, is troubled by this "slaughter of language".

was either so insouciantly having lunch in a bunker underneath, or top leaders were having a meeting ostensibly to plan an attack on American interests. The aggressors apparently acted on intelligence gathering. Intelligence as we know it is largely ambiguous. The "fresh human intelligence"[2] about Saddam's whereabouts could have been of the same quality as the 64,000 outstanding and unassigned leads gathered by FBI's counterterrorism division since 1995.[3]

3. Deceiving Resolutions

Resolution 1441 might well have been a British and U.S. strategy backed in good faith by 13 other Security Council members who thought they were helping to avoid war. France felt good. The resolution did not have the dreaded automatic trigger to war. Bush made it clear war could still be avoided. We Muslims denigrated Syria for backing the Resolution, but Damascus was simply stepping into those diplomatic minefields.

Americans went to the U.N. probably thinking that Saddam would not let the inspectors back in after booting them out four years previously. Chairman of the Joint Chiefs of Staff General Richard Myers inadvertently revealed in April as he bravely defended Donald Rumsfeld over war tactics that the war plan was firmed up back in January and had evolved for longer. The other 13 Security Council members were led to believe Resolution 1441 was a show of force not to lead to the use of force without a Second Resolution. The Americans were ready for war all along. Their troops were

---

2 Which was how the Americans described the tip-off they received.

3 Malcolm Gladwell, "Connecting the Dots", *The New Yorker*, March 10, 2003

rushed to the Middle East ostensibly to browbeat the Iraqis into compliance as diplomats and arms inspectors tried to avoid war.

Blair promised the Second Resolution to Parliament then squirmed, saying unreasonable threat of veto had made war inevitable, and seeking to legitimise war. Robin Cook, who was forced to choose between his wife and mistress by Blair's spin doctors in 1997 when he was Foreign Secretary, wrote that he saluted Blair's efforts to seek a Second Resolution, but said it was wrong to accuse France. Russia, Germany, and many others too opposed the war.

U.N. Secretary-General Kofi Annan said going to war without the authority of the Security Council was unlawful. Jemima Khan, daughter of the late Sir James Goldsmith and wife of Imran Khan, said she was ashamed and angry to be British. She wrote: "Why has Blair chosen to overlook, and, in some cases propagate the lies, misinformation and discredited evidence used by the U.S. to justify the indefensible war." Indian author Arundhati Roy, winner of the 1997 Booker Prize for *The God of Small Things*, tore into manipulations by the U.K. and U.S. She found what she called the "slaughter of language" absurd, and reminded everyone that this exercise was supposed to be about defending America![4]

4. Preventive, Not Pre-emptive Strike

I say when two opposing forces have been getting ready for war and one side fires the first salvo that is indeed a pre-emptive strike. When the aggressor starts pounding on a target that has no intention of striking the opponent and has

4 Arundhati Roy, "Mesopotamia. Babylon. The Tigris and Euphrates," *The Guardian*, April 2, 2003

announced to the world that it has no such intention, that is a preventive strike. The U.S.-U.K. attack on Iraq was an unprovoked strike.

I believe the strike on Iraq has dangerously changed the concept of "self-defence"—nations may just decide to attack another on impulse, citing some vaguely perceived "future threats." German had in the World War II attacked its neighbours in a preventive strike, after which the Nuremberg Trial of 1946 ruled: "To initiate a war of aggression is not only an international crime; it is the supreme international crime differing only from the other war crimes in that it contains within itself the accumulated evil of the whole."

Should American and British military planners and political leaders be brought to justice for all the civilian deaths for using cluster bombs?

5. Illegal Occupation

It is bewildering that France, Russia and Germany plus the U.N. Secretary-General had to talk about the reconstruction of Iraq when they opposed, sometimes, bitterly the war. Businesses talk about contracts as the children were being killed. Morality was trampled upon.

The upshot is the war was illegal and that is an unshakeable truth. Britain argued that the authority to use force came from the combined Resolutions 678, 687 and 1441, when 678 was the very Resolution that empowered U.N. "to use all necessary means" (the code for war) to liberate Kuwait after Iraq invaded the country. Now it is Iraq, which is being invaded when the language of 1441 was confined to a dramatically less potent language of "serious consequences".

Resolution 678 was passed in 1990 while Resolution 687 was passed a year later, marking the end of the conflict. How could you invoke that Resolution to start a new conflict? Resolution 687 ordered Iraq to take necessary steps to make its less dangerous, including disarmament.

6. Unmasking Terrorists

The U.S. was upset some Iraqi combatants were not in their uniforms when U.S. Special Forces in Afghanistan and Iraq, too, moved stealthily without their uniforms. The U.S. State Department officially defines terrorism as "premeditated, politically motivated violence propagated against non combatant targets by sub-national groups or clandestine agents..."

America's War for Independence was waged by irregulars; the British said they were terrorists who resorted to sniping. Since 1945, the British have had to battle irregulars in Palestine, Northern Ireland, Malaya and elsewhere. It was perfectly sensible for the Iraqi to stage some sort of guerrilla warfare against a military that is replenished annually through a budget of $400 billion. The Iraqis were fighting for their national survival.

7. Chemical and Biological Weapons

Hans Blix was infamous in Washington. Head of the International Atomic Energy Agency (IAEA), Mohamed El Baradei was criticised for disputing Anglo-America's unsubstantiated claims regarding Iraqi nuclear programme. They alleged that centrifuges found in Iraq were meant for uranium enrichment purposes. They identified sites for inspectors to search but nothing came out of this. They were unhappy that the inspectors were unable to produce a "positive" report. Inspectors had actually destroyed remnants of Saddam's weaponries. Saddam in fact cooperated with Blix's team, but this was dismissed as a "willful charade". Foiled, Washington went on to discredit the U.N., branding it as a senseless debating society.

8. New Meaning of Words

We have been taught new meaning of words. Liberation effectively means "invasion". Die-hard Saddam loyalists mean "Iraqis resisting the invasion". Weapons of Mass Destruction are "weapons that Saddam had in large quantities but forgot to use and the Iraqi Survey Group is leisurely looking for". Free Press means "pro-American newspapers."

9. Post-Saddam

Iraq is for the Iraqis, said Ari Fleischer. Bush said American troops would not remain in the Middle East "for one day longer than is necessary". Back in 1990, his father said: "We seek no advantage for ourselves, nor do we seek to maintain our military forces in Saudi Arabia for one day longer than is necessary." The son contradicts himself by saying "U.S. intends to stay in Iraq as long as needed, but not one day longer." They may remain in Iraq for years.

The Governing Council consists of exiles like Ahmad Chalabi, head of the Iraqi National Congress. Ahmad Chalabi who has been living outside Iraq, is an American favourite who was secretly flown by the U.S. military to southern Iraq. Blair, being more of the PR man than Bush, is worried Chalabi may be branded a puppet. But Wolfowitz is a big fan of Chalabi. Richard Perle and former CIA director James

Woolsey, too, have cultivated Chalabi, making much about his "democratic experience outside Iraq". The new Iraqi Government in whatever form, will be faithfully pro-U.S. Will it be coerced to recognise Israel?

10. Coalition of the Willing

President Bush praised, rather belatedly, Australian forces who fought alongside U.S. and U.K. forces in Iraq. The coalition of the willing looked suspiciously like a gimmick. The Americans could have done it alone. The Dutch government was said to be anxious when one of its air force officers was whisked on to the podium for a media briefing at Centcom HQ in Qatar. The chap was there on other business.

The coalition included what *The New York Times* called "embarrassing company". "Uzbekistan routinely tortures detainees and some have died in custody. Eritrea has ended freedom of the press (I say how about the Americans?) and restricts religious freedom. Azerbaijan arbitrarily detains dissidents and rigs elections. Significantly violations are noted in such other coalition member as Colombia, Dominican Republic, Georgia, Macedonia, Rwanda, Uganda and Ethiopia." In all seven, the overall human rights situation was rated as poor," the newspaper said in a recent editorial.

Some commentators have warned against underestimating George Bush's intellectual prowess. After all, his rise in politics has been miraculous. I agree. It is just that Cheney and the other hawks are old hands. They have been deepening their arguments for decades, especially on the Middle East situation. They had been key intellectual force in the heart of Washington.

And, they are like-minded, enjoying an ideological affinity especially from the time of the final days of the Cold War. On certain issues, even Colin Powell is in the same wavelength as Cheney and company. Remember, the two of them worked closely together during the Gulf War I, when Cheney was Defense Secretary and Powell, Chairman of the Joint Chiefs of Staff.

True that President Bush calls the shots but on the Middle East, on Israel in particular, he is up against some of the biggest hitters in town. The neo-cons have been in and out of the Washington for decades. They share the same convictions. They write newspaper articles. They have a certain clout in right-wing Press. Now they have all flocked back to Washington. They are a potent force. All they need to do is to convince the president, Karl Rove and Condoleeza Rice to come around to their viewpoints. Observed *New York Times* columnist Maureen Dowd (August 6, 2003): "When the neocons want something, they'll get it done, no matter what Bush thinks."

Bush has met Ariel Sharon eight times since becoming president. Why so? Does the Road Map really stand a chance? Will the Palestinians get a fair deal they so desperately needed?

The "cabal" lurks in the White House. Have they changed their positions to suit Bush's enthusiasm for peace? Richard Pearle had in the 1990s urged Binyamin Netanyahu to shred the Oslo accords and denounce the land for peace approach. In short, a current key Pentagon adviser wants the Likud Party to behave in more hawkish manner.

Rumsfeld had since written a note, which according to *The Washington Post*, reflects his astonishing lack of sensitivity for the feelings of the Arabs.

The note said: "There was a war (in 1967), Israel urged neighbouring countries not to get involved ... they all jumped in, and they lost a lot of real estate to Israel in that conflict. In the intervening period, they've made some settlements in some parts of the so-called occupied area, which was the result of a war, which they won."

The hawks have long argued for a sizeable presence of U.S. troops in Arab land. They have secured this which as I have pointed out enhanced Israel's security.

Now, why did Bush send the troops into Iraq? I think his reasons and that of the hawks don't exactly match. Middle East did not appear on Bush's radar screen until Nine-eleven. What will Bush do if things become horribly wrong? Who shall he turn to for advice?

Did Bush have other options on Iraq? The U.N. troops could have been mobilised as a U.N. team put in place democratic institutions, register voters, educate them politically and encourage the formation of political parties.

After six months or so, the U.N. should then conduct a free and fair election, possibly escorted by a U.N. peacekeeping force. This will allow Iraqis to elect the Government of their choice. Ahmad Chalabi and other organisations should participate in the elections. One would argue about the fate of the Ba'ath party. It is no different from the Communist parties in the old Soviet Bloc. They too should have faith in the electoral process. How do you rebuild a country when the existing institutions are demolished, when chaos reigned, when you have planted pain and misery in people's hearts? The flowering of democracy has to be driven by a soft approach.

The route that the U.S. took was opposed by some of America's closest allies and neighbours, Mexico and Canada included. It is rooted in part on the suspicions of the actual intentions of the Americans, one of which is empire building.

This is a question of might is right all over again. The U.S. pretended to bow to international public opinion simply because it thought it could get its way. Once it was obvious there would be resistance, they brushed aside dissent and breached international laws with impunity. Others will be punished promptly for flouting the laws.

Is this the new reality we all have to live with?

September 10, 2003

The author at a Seminar Closing Address on "Developing a System of Islamic Financial Instrument" in Kuala Lumpur.

With Malaysian Prime Minister, Datuk Seri Dr Mahathir Mohamad, during a visit to Saudi Arabia.

With H.E. President of the Republic of Guinea, General Lansana Conte. (Guinea is a member of the U.N. Security Council.)

With H.E. General Pervez Musharraf of the Republic of Pakistan. (Pakistan supported the war in Afghanistan but opposed the Iraq War.)

With H.E. President of Turkey,
Recep Tayyip Erdogan. (Turkey did not allow
the U.S. to attack Iraq from its territory.)

With one of the Somali warlords, Abdinur Darman,
who is likely to be the next President.